A PSALM FOR UNSEEN SERVANTS

HANCE DILBECK

A PSALM FOR UNSEEN SERVANTS

ENCOURAGEMENT FOR QUIET, HIDDEN KINGDOM WORK

Copyright © 2025 by Hance Dilbeck
All rights reserved.
Printed in the United States of America

979-8-3845-2417-5

Published by B&H Publishing Group
Brentwood, Tennessee

Dewey Decimal Classification: 241.4
Subject Heading: CHURCH VOLUNTEERS \ GRATITUDE \ HELPING BEHAVIOR

All Scripture is taken from the Christian Standard Bible. Copyright © 2017 by Holman Bible Publishers. Used by permission. Christian Standard Bible®, and CSB® are federally registered trademarks of Holman Bible Publishers, all rights reserved.

Scripture references marked (ESV) are taken from the English Standard Version. ESV® Text Edition: 2016. Copyright © 2001 by Crossway Bibles, a publishing ministry of Good News Publishers.

Scripture references marked (NIV) are taken from the New International Version®, NIV® Copyright ©1973, 1978, 1984, 2011 by Biblica, Inc.® Used by permission. All rights reserved worldwide.

Scripture references marked (NASB) are taken from the New American Standard Bible®, Copyright © 1960, 1971, 1977, 1995 by The Lockman Foundation. All rights reserved.

Cover design by Faceout Studio, Jeff Miller. Cover image made from images by Andy445/Getty Images, Thichaa/shutterstock, Suchat Maliwan/shutterstock, heapsimages/shutterstock, and LittleMiss/shutterstock.

1 2 3 4 5 6 • 28 27 26 25

Dedication

A man often came to mind as I worked to understand Psalm 134 and the dynamics of serving unseen. His name is John R. Jones, and I dedicate this little book to him.

The Team at GuideStone might find it odd to consider John Jones an unseen servant. He was a key leader at GuideStone for most of his life—the chief operating officer for twenty-five years. John poured out his life serving those who serve the Lord. He worked with integrity of heart and skillfulness of hand, enhancing the financial security and resilience of literally hundreds of thousands of people. But, most people he served have never heard his name or recognized his unique and extraordinary kingdom contribution.

John, thank you for all you have done for me. Thank you for serving unseen.

Contents

Foreword ix

Introduction: High-Risk Occupation 1

Chapter 1: Who Are the Unseen Servants? 13

Chapter 2: A Word for Unseen Servants 27

Chapter 3: The Psalm 51

Chapter 4: How to Serve Well, Unseen 85

Chapter 5: A Special Case of the Seen Unseen: The Pastor's Wife 105

Chapter 6: The Good News for Unseen Servants 119

Afterword 139

Epilogue: Mission:Dignity 145

About the Author 155

Notes 157

Foreword

"Unseen is not synonymous with unimportant. In fact, for the unseen servant, they work without an audience, without applause and without notice. It is vital."
Hance Dilbeck

What a surprising and, at the same time, unsurprising reminder from Hance Dilbeck. Sadly, in the personality-cult culture of today's evangelical world, having the leader of a large evangelical organization be the one to remind us of unseen servants is quite surprising, at least to me. I've seen the lengths to which our evangelical rockstars will go to protect their personal brand and insulate themselves from interaction with those who buy their books, pay for their simulcasts, and make real sacrifices to sit in the crowd to listen to them at their conferences.

Having served smaller congregations, I have personally felt the sting of feeling unseen, especially when trying to invite guest speakers. Often, we were unable to fill the pulpit. And when we could, we still run the risk of people canceling for various reasons. I even recall a time when my three-year-old daughter was nearly ran over at a busy convention center by people who were rushing to see the next big speaker.

Now comes a book from Hance Dilbeck on the unseen people in ministry with hundreds of employees who serve hundreds of thousands of pastors, missionaries, and church and denominational staff members. He's the same Hance Dilbeck who once pastored a large, growing church, and today is welcomed to the pulpits of megachurches and the stages of the largest conferences. So, yes, having a leader like that author a book reminding us of unseen servants is quite surprising, at least to me. Much like my reaction to a book on humility written by a pastor well-known for his pride, *A Psalm for Unseen Servants* would automatically find me the skeptic, were it not that Hance Dilbeck is the author.

Through mutual friends, I have known about Hance and his reputation for many, many years. I have known him personally for well over a decade. And here is what I know: as a pastor, Hance was a shepherd, not a celebrity. As a denominational leader, he is a servant, not a rockstar. As a friend, he never fails to be an encourager, sharing Scripture, voicing prayers, and lending a listening ear. Hance has not lost the humility gained from a humble beginning. And he has not lost the gratitude experienced by a sinner saved by grace. That he sees the unseen servants of the Lord is of no surprise to me, nor is the fact that he wants us all to see them . . . as the Lord sees them.

Who should read *A Psalm for Unseen Servants*? All of us.

This book is a gift to those who serve others while remaining genuinely unseen, as it reminds them of the One who always sees—the One who truly matters. From the church janitor to the missionary in a closed, impoverished country whose story will never be told, even the most humble and sincere servants will have their hearts blessed and guarded by the Scriptures, illustrations, and wisdom in this book.

A Psalm for Unseen Servants is also a gift to the church. Hance reminds us how dependent we are on those faithful unseen servants who, in their love for Christ and His Bride, carry out the work of ministry week after week, year after year, and over a lifetime. He reminds us how the church should express gratitude to them and for them. As Paul states in 1 Corinthians 12, "The eye cannot say to the hand, 'I have no need of you,' nor again the head to the feet, 'I have no need of you'" (v. 21). Indeed, "God arranged the members in the body, each one of them, as he chose" (v. 18). Every faithful servant, regardless of visibility or popularity, is an essential part of the body of Christ.

Not to be left out, *A Psalm for Unseen Servants* is also a gift to leaders, providing a necessary and timely reminder that, as I heard it said long ago, "The ground is level at the foot of the cross." Regardless of one's role or acclaim, we are equals. And we should "do nothing from selfish ambition or conceit, but in humility count others more significant" than ourselves (Phil. 2:3 ESV). Moreover, leaders, like the Church, should be quick to see the unseen servants around them, express gratitude to and for them, and recognize how dependent we are on others to make ministry happen.

No, "Unseen is not synonymous with unimportant." Thank you, Hance Dilbeck, for helping us to see that—and to see those who truly are important.

Paul Chitwood, PhD
President, International Mission Board

Introduction

High-Risk Occupation

Call to Evening Worship
A song of ascents.

Now bless the L*ORD,*
all you servants of the L*ORD*
who stand in the L*ORD's house at night!*
Lift up your hands in the holy place
and bless the L*ORD!*

May the L*ORD,*
Maker of heaven and earth,
bless you from Zion.
Psalm 134

Imagine working on the deck of a commercial fishing boat. The wind and waves rock the boat, every step you take is fraught with potential danger. Nets, booms, winches all constantly threaten harm. You are just trying to make a living, but every day your life is at risk. According to The Pew Charitable Trusts[1] and the FISH Safety Foundation, more than 100,000 commercial fishermen are killed each year worldwide.

Have you ever taken the time to watch the men replacing a roof? They work hard carrying heavy loads, swinging a hammer in the hot sun putting shingles into place. Their work is impressive in its own right, but of course it is all done high above the ground on a steep, slippery surface with no safety net! It is dangerous work.

Go to the tall forests of the Northwest and observe a logger. These modern-day Paul Bunyans do not use a big blue ox. They use fast-moving, powerful machinery—spinning blades, heavy equipment, difficult terrain. And of course, time is always of the essence. The fatality rate among loggers is 82 per 100,000 workers, compared to the average of 7 per 100,000 in the general population.[2]

Fishing, logging, and roofing are high-risk occupations. In fact, the Bureau of Labor Statistics declares them the top three most dangerous occupations year after year.[3]

The thing is, those who enter these occupations know that they are assuming significant risk. Their employers often provide frequent safety demonstrations, reminders, and trainings. These needed workers are fully aware of the dangers of their chosen professions. This book deals with another kind of dangerous work. These occupations come with risks that are much more subtle, yet still quite real. The risks are not usually physical, but more often spiritual.

Consider the risks of working in a religious setting, in a church, or a Christian ministry. Those who work out front in these ministries assume risks of which we are very aware—hypocrisy and pride.

The examples are too numerous to list. The president of the Northern Seminary in Illinois resigned in 2023 after he was accused of bullying and retaliating against staff that brought the matter to trustees.[4] A Florida Roman Catholic Church had a former finance manager plead guilty in federal court to defrauding her local congregation of $775,000.[5] Some leaders falsify their credentials to obtain more prestige and higher positions. Others divert church resources to their personal bank account. Let's not leave out the scourge of sex abuse that has rightly ended many ministry careers. Most of us have read multiple media reports on similar matters and it makes our hearts break for the impact on the kingdom and for the victims.

But what about the men and women who work behind the scenes? Are there unique risks for those who serve unseen?

We all know that behind every successful church or ministry there is an army of workers who labor far from the limelight. They do the work to ensure the books are balanced, the livestream goes off without a hitch, to make sure the musicians can be heard—but not too loudly!—amidst the congregation, who ensure the facilities are ready week in and week out and (much to the doubt of many in the sanctuary) that the building is neither too hot nor too cold.

Most people begin working in a church or Christian ministry ***because they are committed to the Lord, believe in His work, and want to work in a more pleasant or protected environment. They love the Lord, love the people, and love the work***. These are folks who quickly learn that their church staff is made up of flawed people too! These occupations are viewed as safe, sheltered, and free from the pressures and temptations found in the secular workplace or the corporate culture. That is partially true, of course. Working in a church or ministry is a special calling as unto the Lord. But human beings *are* human beings. Flawed people exist in the church office, just as they do anywhere else. Because of that, subtle dangers lurk.

The unseen servant might not struggle with hypocrisy or pride and all their ugly fruit, but what about a root of bitterness?

When we serve unseen, behind the scenes, we can begin to feel unappreciated, or worse, even completely unnoticed. Over the years, our work that began with a strong sense of service to the Lord becomes disconnected from the Lord. We do our work without any sense of His presence or His pleasure. Also, work that we once viewed as having vital connection to the kingdom of God becomes very ordinary and disconnected from biblical mission. Worst of all, though, while we begin serving with a deep love for the people of God, this feeling of being unappreciated often creates a bitterness toward the people we serve. We no longer love them; in fact, we resent them. "If only the church didn't have all these people, I could get my work done!" It's easy to forget *why* we do what we do. Our bitterness can build barriers that keep us from connecting our work with our Lord, His mission, and His people.

Consider some unseen servants found on the pages of Holy Scripture.

I love the story of Martha and Mary told in Luke's Gospel. Jesus has been teaching around the countryside, and in verse 38 of Luke 10, Jesus enters a village and Martha welcomes the Messiah into her home. Martha and Mary, of course, have a famous brother, Lazarus, whom Jesus would raise from the dead. Martha was hosting the King of kings, the Lord of lords, the Son of the Most High, so she did what any reasonable unseen servant would do: She got distracted by her many tasks.

Jesus had an entourage—twelve disciples who came along with Him. Likely, she was busy preparing a meal fit for the King and His followers. She wanted to make sure the house was presentable to them.

Her sister, Mary, though, didn't worry about the preparation. Instead, Mary "sat at the Lord's feet and was listening to what he said" (v. 39). It's hard not to have this image in your mind's eye. Martha was likely agitated and finally called upon the Lord, "Don't you care that my sister has left me to serve alone? So tell her to give me a hand" (v. 40).

Put yourself in Martha's shoes for a moment. Was she being unreasonable? Likely, you're thinking Martha has made an absolutely reasonable request.

How does Jesus respond?

> The Lord answered her, "Martha, Martha, you are worried and upset about many things, but one thing is necessary. Mary has made the right choice, and it will not be taken away from her." (Luke 10:41–42)

Martha was serving unseen and had become bitter. Her work *was* vital. If people are to be fed, someone has to prepare the ingredients, get it into the oven on time, and make sure the table is set. But she lost sight of the most important ingredient: the Lord Himself. He's fed 5,000 on a hillside with nothing more than a boy's lunch of loaves and fish. He could handle supper for sixteen people.

Consider the older son. We know his story as The Parable of the Prodigal Son, who went off and wasted his part of the inheritance on lavish and wasteful living. The father waited each day to see if his prodigal would return. He finally did, only after spending all of his inheritance and had hired himself out and was starving. The prodigal was repentant and was even willing to be a slave to his father, who instead put a ring on his finger, a robe on his back, and sandals on his feet. Then he had the fattened calf slaughtered for a barbeque feast.

The older son has been working diligently for his father, staying faithful to his calling. He served unseen, and as the responsible child, did everything required of him. So, as he comes home, he sees there is a celebration and asks one of the servants what is happening. He is told the good news; his brother is back safe and sound.

For the older brother, however, it's not good news. "He became angry and didn't want to go in. So his father came out and pleaded with him" (Luke 15:28). The older brother, like many unseen servants, focused on his service, his sacrifice, his obedience, and his needs. He couldn't see the great news the younger brother's return actually was, even referring to *his* brother as "this son of *yours*" (v. 30, emphasis mine).

Bitterness is real. It can grow and fester if we don't regularly check our spirits. It can also lead to outright disobedience.

Gehazi was Elisha's trusted aid and servant. In 2 Kings 5, we see the fruit of bitterness revealed. The story is familiar: Naaman, a commander in Syria's army, was a "valiant warrior" (v. 1), but he had a skin disease. An Israelite slave told Naaman's wife that he should go to the prophet in Samaria who could heal him. Naaman received permission from Syria's king to go to Israel with a letter to Israel's king, to seek out Elisha to be healed. Second Kings 5:5 said Naaman went with 750 pounds of silver, 150 pounds of gold, and ten sets of clothing. Once Naaman came to Elisha, the prophet told him to go wash seven times in the Jordan River and his skin would be restored. It took a bit of convincing, but Naaman did as he was told. And when he was clean with "the skin of a small boy," he returned to Elisha to offer a gift, saying, "I know there's no God in the whole world except in Israel." Elisha refused the gifts.

Gehazi couldn't believe it. Elisha has let this Syrian off lightly in Gehazi's mind. So he spiritualizes the decision, runs after him, and lies, asking for 75 pounds of silver (one-tenth of what Naaman had) and two sets of clothing. Naaman is so overjoyed by being healed, he insists Gehazi take 150 pounds of silver and two servants to carry it. Gehazi drops the silver off at his house and dismisses the servants, and then returns to Elisha.

Elisha asks where he's been. Gehazi lies again, and Naaman pronounces a curse saying that Naaman's skin diseases would cling to Gehazi and his descendants forever.

Unseen service can lead to bitterness and covetousness. But ultimately, it can lead to disobedience. This should cause us to shudder and pause to ensure our hearts are right before the Lord.

This book is written for those serving unseen, behind the scenes, in churches and ministries. For the older brothers, the Marthas, and the Gehazis among us.

We will use a little psalm from the Old Testament to highlight the importance of unseen service and the keys to protecting ourselves from the subtle hypocrisy of bitterness. You might never have noticed this psalm in your devotional readings, or maybe never fully understood its significance. I hope this provides some comfort that close to the center of the Bible is a psalm with unseen servants in mind.

These servants will likely never be invited to headline a conference. Their work may not seem "spiritual" to everybody. But it's likely that their work would be missed if they didn't do it week in and week out. Let this be a reminder for the pastors who serve the unseen servants, and let this be an encouragement to those who serve unseen!

Chapter 1

Who Are the Unseen Servants?

Call to Evening Worship

A song of ascents.

Now bless the LORD,
all you servants of the LORD
who stand in the LORD's house at night!
Lift up your hands in the holy place
and bless the LORD!

May the LORD,
Maker of heaven and earth,
bless you from Zion.
Psalm 134

In the 2016 movie *Hidden Figures*, we are introduced to three African-American female mathematicians serving at NASA. During the peak of the space race between the United States and the former Soviet Union, these women served as the brains behind getting John Glenn into space, becoming the first man to orbit the Earth, and bringing him safely home. They worked diligently to help ensure NASA's successes in the 1960s, in fact. Sadly, most of us were unaware of their vital contributions for a half-century.

These "human computers," Dorothy Vaughan, Mary Jackson, and Katherine Gobels Johnson, played an important role in the space race that ultimately led to the United States being the first to land a man safely on the moon and bring him back to Earth first. Despite the racial challenges and hostility of that turbulent decade, they worked tirelessly to contribute to the success of the space race.

Their role was vital, yet unseen. *Unseen* is not a synonym for *unimportant* or *unworthy*.

When you go to the movies, do you ever sit in the theater to watch the credits? There are incredible stars that shine on the silver screen whose names appear immediately after the closing scene, but they could not exhibit their acting gifts were it not for the hundreds of men and women behind the scenes. Cameramen, sound technicians, extras, costume designers, directors, composers, editors, photographers, producers, writers, production managers, stuntmen, choreographers, artists, publishers, even accountants and lawyers. These all get their names in the credits. Why? Well, even though they're unseen, that two-hour movie could not happen without them. While there may have been a handful of key actors, their work never would have been on the screen without the dedication of people who labor unseen.

The same is true for your church and mine.

When most members talk about a church service, they primarily think of the pastor and worship leader. They might consider an age-graded minister (children's director or youth minister, for example). But if your church is one of size, Sunday morning worship relies on a host of people in the background—volunteers, of course, but also paid staff that serve behind the bright lights. They are often unnoticed unless there is a problem.

Most weeks, they serve unseen.

When I was a seminary student, I served a small, rural congregation in Oklahoma as their pastor. My wife and I were in our early twenties, and we lived in the parsonage next to the church. Our first son was just old enough to walk from the parsonage to church. Our lives were busy. She worked as a nurse nearby to keep food on the table while I commuted to Southwestern Baptist Theological Seminary in Fort Worth, Texas, to study three days a week. Most Saturday afternoons and early evenings, I found myself in my study at the church preparing for Sunday worship.

On Saturdays, only one other person was in the church building: Harold. Harold had retired from Dallas to a lake nearby. He was an active member of our little church and he had agreed to be the custodian. We paid him a small amount each week and he gave us far more than our money's worth.

While I wrote my sermon and used a typewriter to create the Sunday order of service (yes, *a typewriter*, I am that old!), Harold set up chairs, vacuumed the carpet, and cleaned the bathrooms. His last task was very important to this faithful servant. He spent a considerable amount of time cleaning the front door to the church, a glass door. Harold was meticulous when it came to that door. He wanted everyone who walked in the next morning to know that he had done his job. He felt it reflected properly on the importance of the entire gathering.

Well, Harold had a problem—the pastor's firstborn son! When I stayed too late on Saturday, my son would toddle over to tell me it was time to come home. When he did, before his mother could intervene, he would invariably reach up and put his hand on that clean glass door. Now, Harold's masterpiece was ruined with a handprint. It may have been a cute little handprint, but the culprit was obvious.

I can still see Harold's smile in my mind's eye. He would pat the preacher's kid on the head and go get his Windex.

I have deep respect for Mr. Harold. Even as I write these words, I recall his hard work, as unto the Lord. He served well. He served in a vital role. And few people ever seemed to notice him even though he made sure our members had a clean, stocked, and sanitary place to gather in worship to the Lord.

This book is written for men and women like him.

These unseen servants can be found supporting every local church and Christian ministry. They are often unnoticed, in fact most of them prefer to be out of the spotlight. They are too often unappreciated as their faithful work is taken for granted.

Consider the nursery worker. She shows up early to prepare the room and receive the children. She makes young parents feel comfortable and manages the room. She is Bible teacher, comforter, and corrector. Part educator, part psychologist, part custodian. Most people do not know her name, but for a few she is the first person that comes to mind when they think of the church, even before the pastor or worship leader. In fact, many of the young families in your church only joined because of that nursery worker's loving care that made them feel secure in leaving their child.

And we all know a church secretary or administrative assistant who plays a vital role in the work of the Lord. The first voice on the phone representing the church to the community. A vital force holding all the parts together in a cohesive unit. She typically knows everything happening in the church, and usually the history behind it. (The wise pastor knows to make friends with a godly church secretary!) This person does not get top billing—her name might not be on the church's website—but she can set the tone for so much of the ministry. Administrator, counselor, confidante—this person is often the first one to be seen in a church or ministry office, yet somehow unseen when it is time to recognize key contributors.

What about the man in the sound booth? Here is a servant no one sees, until he makes a mistake, and every head turns!

The goal of this servant is to be unnoticed. If he does his job well—aided by the computers that often have minds of their own—no one thinks of him. He is not in the spotlight, but sometimes, literally, behind the spotlight so that others can be seen or heard or understood. Most churches and ministries today could not function without those who work in media. Yet, these essential servants are often unappreciated or at the very least, unnoticed. Of course, until a microphone's volume is too high or the pastor's notes do not show up on the screen.

Do you know who unlocks your church building every Sunday morning? Who turns on the lights? In a smaller church, it's often the pastor. But, in many churches, it's a deacon, custodian, or other worker. These are unseen servants.

Many pastors serve far from the spotlight. They work without any support staff and preach for only a handful of people. When this pastor goes to the church office, he is all alone. He doesn't have an administrative assistant or a media ministry. He is the media ministry! He is the one who unlocks the church, turns on the lights, and later, who turns off the lights and locks up the church. Much of this pastor's work is largely unseen.

We could go on and on with the list of unseen servants in churches and ministry. Men and women providing food service, security, parking assistance, transportation. Their work is very different, but they share a common bond. They provide essential, faithful service that is behind the scenes and often hidden, forgotten (until something goes wrong), unappreciated, and unacknowledged. None of this is out of malice, of course. The work is vital, but often forgotten. Unseen.

What does the Bible have to say about unseen servants?

In the Old Testament, we find the Levites serving unseen. The Levites were the lowest of the three orders in Israel's priesthood. Notice: They were not unimportant, unvalued, or unappreciated. They just were not front and center. They didn't stand in the spotlight. The Levites assisted the priests. They worked behind the scenes preparing offerings, purifying instruments for use in the temple worship, maintaining the temple. These servants were craftsmen, musicians, treasurers, and gatekeepers. Worship in the temple was functionally impossible without the Levites' work. Consider this text as a description of the Levitical service:

> The four chief gatekeepers, who were Levites, were entrusted with the rooms and the treasuries of God's temple. They spent the night in the vicinity of God's temple, because they had guard duty and were in charge of opening it every morning. (1 Chron. 9:26–27)

The Levites were not standing on a platform and pronouncing the benediction. They were not taking the lead role in offering sacrifices. They were behind-the-scenes servants who kept the temple worship going.

The unseen servants aren't just an Old Testament phenomenon. They are an essential part of both Jesus's and Paul's ministries. In the New Testament, we find repeated reference to a group of women who supported Jesus. Some of them are named, but others are not. These women are not recognized like the twelve apostles, but clearly their ministries were essential.

> Afterward he was traveling from one town and village to another, preaching and telling the good news of the kingdom of God. The Twelve were with him, and also some women

> who had been healed of evil spirits and sicknesses: Mary, called Magdalene (seven demons had come out of her); Joanna the wife of Chuza, Herod's steward; Susanna; and many others who were supporting them from their possessions. (Luke 8:1–3)

Isn't that phrase striking: "and many others who were supporting." Unseen servants are almost always also unnamed. The Gospels teach us that from the beginning, from the early days of Jesus's ministry, this group of women supported the advance of the gospel. This is still true today.

In every ministry there are people in lead roles, like the Twelve. We know their names; they are upfront and visible. Their work, too, is vital. They are often recognized for their talent, their faithfulness, and their sacrifices. In every church and ministry there are also "many others who are contributing." These women were among the first unseen servants of Christian ministry.

At the close of Paul's letter to Rome, we find a list of people. Paul knew them by name, but very few know them today. These are not well-known, nor famous. These early

Christian servants are seldom celebrated; but Paul understood the kingdom value of quiet behind-the-scenes service. He names twenty-eight people!

Phoebe

Priscilla

Aquila

Epaenetus

Mary

Andronicus

Junia

Ampliatus

Urbanus

Stachys

Apelles

The household of Aristobulus

Herodion

The household of Narcissus

Tryphaena

Tryphosa

Persis

Rufus

Asyncritus

Phlegon

Hermes

Patrobas

Hermas

Philologus

Julia

Nereus and his sister

Olympas

The church depends on people like those named here. Servants, helpers, hosts, and workers. These roles are not glamorous, but they are essential.

Here is the Bible truth: There is a special glory to unseen service.

This volume is a chance to remind everyone of the importance of the unseen servant. It can be frustrating to serve when no one notices you—unless something goes wrong! It can be easy to become bitter when your contributions are not celebrated. But take heart! I have good news for you: your Father, "who sees in secret" is taking note; He is aware, and He is honored by your faithful, fervent service to Him.

Remember Mr. Harold, the church custodian at my first pastorate? It's likely people came to church who didn't give thought to his work. But if he missed a week, or only did a lackadaisical job, forgetting to stock a restroom or clean a sink or carpet, people would have learned just how valuable his role was.

Thank God for unseen servants who serve well!

Chapter 2

A Word for Unseen Servants

Call to Evening Worship
A song of ascents.

Now bless the L*ORD*,
all you servants of the L*ORD*
who stand in the L*ORD's house at night!*
Lift up your hands in the holy place
and bless the L*ORD!*

May the L*ORD*,
Maker of heaven and earth,
bless you from Zion.
Psalm 134

There are certain career fields that most of us give very little thought to—at least until those workers are not available. Such was the case in 1981 when New York City garbage collectors went on strike. Most of us don't think twice about garbage workers, as essential as their work is. We simply roll the trash bin or carry the trash bags to the curb, and at some point in the day, men riding in specially equipped trucks come by and haul our waste to the landfill. We bring the empty bins back to the garage or alleyway.

On December 1, 1981, New York's sanitation workers went on strike. And the trash bags immediately started piling up in the sidewalks of Manhattan. "We certainly can't stand the trash around, and people have to find a place to walk in the street," one woman told a local television station.[6] Fortunately for New Yorkers, the strike ended December 17 and workers collected the trash and life returned to normal.

Unseen service is not irrelevant service. In fact, it is usually vital service that would create a significant vacuum if it weren't done well, even if it's not front-of-mind for everybody. New Yorkers were quick to notice when the trash wasn't picked up. Your role is valuable in its own right to your church or ministry.

As we reflect on unseen service, Paul offers some important insight at the end of his letter to Rome. Paul mentions several individuals who were serving Christ in the center of the known world. Twenty-eight were already there and one, Phoebe, had recently arrived with his letter.

Phoebe is called a servant. She was evidently a woman of considerable wealth and social position, a patron of the church. Phoebe was from Cenchrea, a port city of Corinth, so it is likely she had arranged hospitality and support for many traveling gospel messengers. Paul commended Phoebe to the church at Rome and encouraged them to give her the support that she deserved.

Priscilla and Aquila are the first people Paul greets in Rome. This power couple is mentioned several times in the New Testament. Paul expresses deep gratitude for them. He calls them "fellow workers" and we recall their time together making tents and preaching the gospel. Acts 18 gives the account:

> After this, he left Athens and went to Corinth, where he found a Jew named Aquila, a native of Pontus, who had recently come from Italy

> with his wife Priscilla because Claudius had ordered all the Jews to leave Rome. Paul came to them, and since they were of the same occupation, tentmakers by trade, he stayed with them and worked. (Acts 18:1–3)

Priscilla is usually mentioned first, Priscilla and Aquila. She may have had more social status, or maybe she was simply a strong woman. This couple seems to have had some financial stability; maybe they owned their own business in Rome. They were forced to leave Rome for a season because of religious persecution, but now they have returned.

The Acts account helps us understand why Paul describes Priscilla and Aquila as "fellow workers" (Rom. 16:3 ESV). They had worked together making tents in Corinth, and worked together proclaiming the gospel of Jesus, making disciples, planting churches. As Jewish Christians living in the Roman world, this couple often encountered risk: hostility from the Jewish kinsmen, from local leaders, and from the Roman authorities.

Now Priscilla and Aquila are back in Rome. They have opened their home to host and likely lead a house church. The

Lord used this couple in a profound way as the gospel spread from Jerusalem to Rome, but most today do not know their names.

Paul loved Epaenetus (v. 5). This saint had known Christ longer than most. In fact, Paul says that he was the first to convert to Christianity from Asia, likely a reference to the west coast of Asia Minor, modern-day Turkey. All roads lead to Rome; for some reason, Epaenetus had left his home and found his way to Rome. He is still faithfully serving Christ.

"Greet Mary" (v. 6). Mary is obviously a common Jewish name. Paul commends her for her hard work. Paul is not using vocabulary that speaks to a specific title or task, but a woman who is willing to take on a difficult task, to toil or struggle in the work. Notice that Mary was working hard, "for you." She worked to serve her brothers and sisters in Rome.

Andronicus and Junia are Greek names, but Paul calls them his kinsmen; so, they were likely Hellenized Jews. James D. G. Dunn, in the *Word Biblical Commentary: Romans 9–16*, declares that "The most natural way to read the two names within the phrase is as husband and wife."[7] This couple had been imprisoned for following Jesus at some point. Maybe even in the same prison with Paul.

You have probably never heard of Andronicus and Junia, but Paul tells us two interesting facts about them. Firstly, they were some of the earliest disciples of Jesus, preceding even Paul. Secondly, they were "outstanding among the apostles" (v. 7 NIV). We are not sure exactly what this means, but it may be a reference to the fact that they had seen the resurrected Christ—eyewitnesses! (1 Cor. 15: 6–7). It certainly puts these Hellenistic Jews among the earliest converts that we read about in the first six chapters of Acts.

Again, we are reminded of how little we know about those faithful servants who carry out the Lord's work. Most, it seems, do so unseen.

Ampliatus, Urbanus, and Stachys are all mentioned with reference to working together and love (Rom. 16:8–9). All three are common slave names.

Apelles is "approved in Christ" (v. 10). This might be a general reference to his maturity; he is respected by the other Christians. It could also be a more specific reference to some particular trial he had endured. He stood the test with his character refined and revealed. Of course, we have no way of knowing the specific nature of the trial, but the church in Rome would likely have known.

Next comes the name Aristobulus (v. 10). But Paul's reference is to his household, not the man. In fact, the man could have already been dead. He was probably a Jewish man with considerable status who put it all at risk to follow Jesus. Many of the slaves and freedmen in his household were influenced by his faith and also came to Christ. Herodion was likely a slave or freedman from Herod's family, maybe somehow associated with the household of Aristobulus (v. 11).

The fact that the household of Narcissus receives a greeting, but not Narcissus himself, likely indicates that he was no longer living but he had influenced many in his household to become Christians. Tryphaena and Tryphosa were likely sisters, actively working for Jesus in Rome, along with Persis, another hard worker whom Paul loved. Persis is called "the beloved" (v. 12 ESV), not "my beloved." This might be because she was widely loved, or because Paul was avoiding an overly familiar expression to a woman.

The fact that we find Rufus and his mother in Rome is fascinating (v. 13). Remember that Mark likely wrote his gospel while in Rome. He mentions Rufus by name: "And they led Him out to crucify Him. They pressed into service a passer-by coming from the country, Simon of Cyrene (the father of Alexander and Rufus), to bear His cross" (Mark 15:20b–21 NASB). Now, Rufus was a fairly common name, and this may have been a totally different man, but the reference to his mother seems to be a reference to his family. This leaves us with so many questions.

Is this the widow and son of the man, Simon, who carried the cross of Jesus? Is that why Paul calls him a "choice man in the Lord" (Rom. 16:13 NASB)? Can you imagine the stories they could tell, stories they heard directly from Simon? How did they come to live in Rome? Did the mother of Rufus, the wife of Simon, support Paul in some other season of ministry, maybe defend him in Jerusalem? Is that why he calls her his mother?

This list reminds us that there is much we do not know about the way men and women serve Jesus.

Paul has more people to recognize, but he needs to pick up the pace: Asyncritus, Phlegon, Hermes, Patrobas, and Hermas (v. 14). These are all names of men who were likely slaves or former slaves. The reference to the brethren with them might be a reference to one house church in Rome.

Dunn suggests that Philologus, Julia, Nereus, and his sister might be members of one family: father, mother, son, and daughter. Along with Olympas, they were gathered as a house church. The names give some indication they might be slaves in the emperor's household.[8] Yet they dared to confess Jesus as Lord.

I thank God for this list of faithful servants. I wish we knew more about them. One day, when we get to heaven, we shall know more. It is important that we make an observation about the list as a whole. This is a diverse group of people. The descriptions and the names themselves give us insight. Both men and women were serving Jesus in important ways. Christ elevates the status of women, and they were serving, working, and leading in ways that Paul did not ignore. Phoebe and Priscilla are acknowledged as important leaders. In fact, consider the following facts from Paul's list:

- At least nine of the twenty-eight people mentioned in verses 3–16 are women.
- Three of the first five people Paul mentions are women.
- All four recognized for their hard work are women.

Paul mentions men and women. Paul mentions Jews and Gentiles. Several are his kinsmen, fellow Jews who had come to know Christ as the Messiah, their Lord. Most are Gentiles.

All are his brothers and sisters in Christ.

All roads lead to Rome, so the Jews and Gentiles had come from a wonderful variety of backgrounds. Yet, we find them all serving Christ together in Rome.

Notice also that Paul acknowledges Christians with a wide variety of social status. Some had high status and wealth; they carried financial power and social influence. Some were freedmen, former slaves who lived with independence. Many seem to have been slaves. Slavery in the Roman world was different from the evils of chattel slavery in early American history, yet slaves still had few rights. We can easily say they were the at the bottom of the social ladder. But in Christ, they are fellow workers, brothers, sisters, beloved.

Paul uses important words in reference to these servants. Most are obscure, almost all unknown, unseen by us. Yet, consider the text: *Commend*, *receive*, *help*, *greet*, *give thanks*, *love*, and *kiss*. Seven verbs that all speak to one common call for the church: acknowledge those who are serving Jesus in your midst.

Four Ways to Acknowledge Others

Acknowledge is a powerful word. "To recognize the rights, authority or status of; to express gratitude or obligation for."[9] Paul models that art of recognition. He shows us how easy, yet how powerful, it is when we acknowledge those who are working hard serving Jesus and His church. Paul teaches four basic elements of effective recognition.

1. Recognize People for Their Deeds

Time is short for Paul and this acknowledgment list is compressed. However, he makes the time to mention the specific activities of many servants. Paul seems particularly interested in hard work, hospitality, and service. These three activities sustain ministry in the kingdom. The people who stand in front of the room to lead worship and proclaim God's Word each Sunday are infinitely valuable. But a church or ministry will not last long, regardless of the quality of the men behind the pulpit, without the saints who are willing to serve faithfully behind the scenes. You may have one who preaches in a way that is faithful and piercing while drawing great multitudes like Adrian Rogers, W. A. Criswell, or Charles Spurgeon. But the crowds won't keep coming if there are no audio people to project the sound, financial secretaries to count and deposit the offering, or if there are no janitors ensuring well-stocked and clean, sanitary restrooms.

Consider hospitality as the epitome of unseen service. Hospitality is a theme in this list of servants and service. Hospitality takes time and money. It is often unappreciated, yet hospitality is essential for the church to gather, to fellowship, and to grow together. Those who serve the church by preparing a room, preparing their home, preparing a meal, and making people feel welcomed are practicing hospitality. These unseen servants ought to be acknowledged with gratitude and respect.

As a pastor, I came to church early on Sunday morning and left late. But somehow, there were always some people there before me and some dear saints who left after me. They were working hard, serving behind the scenes, preparing and providing hospitality—food service, custodians, nursery workers.

Ministry is hard work. Paul mentions this repeatedly and every faithful servant of Christ's church would say a loud

Amen! Committed Christian servants work hard. Sometimes a well-meaning church member will comment about how wonderful it must be to serve vocationally in a church—as if it's only preaching and meeting members for lunch! I don't know why it surprises us when serving in a church or ministry is difficult. We have an Enemy, and it's not the deacons or the finance committee. Satan will be there to attack us. The father of lies will sow bitterness and greed, which will affect the work. That makes it hard work. I once served with a minister of music who referred to Christian ministry simply as "the work." No matter what your role, it is work; and often it will be hard. But still, there is a glory in hard work.

Pastors should remember the unseen servants in multi-staff churches. It can be easy to be lulled into complacency when a great team surrounds you. The food service team ensures the coffee is tasty, hot, and in the right place at the right time each week. Meals for key meetings are ready at the right time and in the right quantity. The nursery workers are ready to go when the first child arrives. The A/V staff, working with a system held together with duct tape and bailing wire, continues to excel. It can quickly become easy to just take their work for granted; that they are just "doing their job." And while it is true that they are doing their job—and should want to do their job with excellence—as managers, it is important to recognize the work of those rowing *with* the team just as we would seek to correct those rowing *against* the team

2. Recognize the Details of Their Service

No doubt, there were many details of which Paul is clearly unaware. His travels, his writing, his time in prison all meant that he would be unaware of some of the work. Some of these saints receive a kind of blanket recognition. But, when Paul knew some detail of their service, he put it in the spotlight. Phoebe had helped Paul; Priscilla and Aquila had risked their own necks; Epaenetus was the first convert in Asia; Mary worked hard. Paul mentions details.

When we mention details, we let people know we are paying attention to their work—which is often surprising to them that we noticed. Acknowledging details is a powerful way to say, "Your work matters." The unseen servant often grows discouraged when she suspects no one really appreciates her extra effort or remarkable consistency. When we mention details, we are saying, "We see you."

Pastors who see someone every week serving the Lord should mention it! Is there a team member prayer-walking the parking lot before the service, picking up any trash that has blown in? Tell them! Everyone appreciates being acknowledged. (That said, it's important for us all to know our team as people. I've known some who would be horrified to be recognized from the platform, but that doesn't mean I couldn't thank them one-on-one.)

3. Recognize Others Through Affection

Paul expresses true love for these servants. He often calls them "beloved." He uses family language: "brother," "sister," even "mother." He even encourages some physical expression of true affection in Romans 16:16, "Greet one another with a holy kiss." (By the way, I would highly recommend you only do that last one if your wife is the church worker you're celebrating!)

Expressing affection is not easy for some of us. Serving among weathered men, I encountered more than one who defended their lack of affection by saying, "I told my wife I loved her the day we married. If that ever changes, she'll be the first to know." Many a manager has made the mistake of saying, "If you don't hear from me, you're doing fine in the work." If we are truly observing the faithful service of others, we will find a natural affection for them—perhaps a *supernatural* affection. God's Spirit stirs us up to love them. Express that love in word and deed. Acknowledgment is affection expressed.

4. Call a Servant by His or Her Name

Most of all, Paul demonstrates the one fundamental element of effective recognition. It is the very essence of recognition: Paul names names.

There is power in calling a person by her name. There is power when a well-loved leader publicly recognizes a person by name or privately greets a servant by name. To name names means we know them. To know names means we value a person. Imagine how these saints felt when this letter was read in church and their names were called out loud.

When we call someone by name, we convey intimacy and respect. To know someone's name is to say, "I care about you. I see your work, and you are important!" Of course, the inverse is also true. When we fail to learn the name of someone who serves the church week after week, when we fail to call that faithful person by his or her name, we send a not-so-subtle message: "I don't care about you. I don't see your work, and you are not really all that important."

Calling people by name is important in every arena of life. We should want to know the names of our neighbors, those we encounter in commerce, or in the community. But, above all, we must use the names of those who serve alongside us in ministry. If you are not calling a fellow servant by name, you are not recognizing him or her. Using their name shows respect and acknowledges their value. It is not that complicated. Say their name.

Two Types of Acknowledgment: Formal and Informal

Formal Recognition

We call someone up on a platform and give them a plaque or a gift. We applaud together as we recognize their service. This is often a special occasion, an anniversary, or some other milestone. Of course, these times of formal recognition are important.

At GuideStone, where I serve as president and chief executive officer, we have opportunities to formally recognize our employees. Let me offer you two ways to prime the pump to consider in your own context.

John R. Jones is one of the most amazing, influential Southern Baptists, but you likely wouldn't know him since he, too, often served unseen. For thirty-five years, John served GuideStone faithfully—twenty-five of those years he served as chief operating officer, first under my predecessor, O. S. Hawkins, and then me. John had the fortune—or misfortune perhaps!—of serving under four different GuideStone presidents, including also Darold Morgan and Paul Powell as the head of the investments division. He came to what was then the Annuity Board of the Southern Baptist Convention from the banking and insurance world. He was not a preacher or a missionary, but he knew God had called him to our ministry enterprise to serve pastors and missionaries. When I arrived at GuideStone, one of my key prayers was to have a productive relationship with John Jones. I am thankful God answered that prayer affirmatively and count John as a trusted counselor and friend.

Listen to how my predecessor, O. S. Hawkins, described him at John's retirement reception: "He is highly relational. Every employee feels seen and heard by John; he cares deeply for people inside GuideStone, and for those GuideStone is privileged to serve. His heart for Mission:Dignity[10] is contagious. He cares about the 'pastor at the crossroads' who labors in often forgotten places, faithfully laboring out of the spotlight for the Lord."

When I arrived at GuideStone, I (like a lot of people) struggled for the right word to describe our *enterprise*, the ultimate word we landed on. At this writing, GuideStone has more than $20 billion in assets under management. We have a tremendous compliance team, legal team, finance and accounting professionals. Every email I receive seems to have some combination of letters after the names in the signature: CFP, CPA, CRPC, CEBS, SHRM-CP, and more. But for all of the professionals (all of whom I'm thankful for), these are also people who are focused on ministry as well, caring for many unseen servants through Mission:Dignity or laboring in lonely roles throughout the country and around the world. Everyone shares the common faith of those we serve.

For John, that dichotomy of church and ministry was the beauty of GuideStone. Every employee who knew him could repeat his well-worn line: *GuideStone is a ministry guided by best business practices.* I love that phrase. It meant our enterprise is both ministry and business. Primarily, we are a ministry enterprise, but we do so with the wisdom and prudence of good business managers—we get to be the best of both worlds!

To celebrate John's tenure, it was our privilege in 2024 to introduce the first-ever John R. Jones Enterprise Excellence Award given to one staff member. This recognition is given to an employee who demonstrates a heart for both our ministry and our business needs. In 2024, we awarded it to Dustin Sanders. Dustin's name will be familiar to our International Mission Board (IMB) staff. A former missionary himself, Dustin serves the retirement planning needs of the IMB staff, both at its headquarters in Richmond, Virginia, and around the world. Dustin is not one who needs to be in the limelight, though the Lord has gifted Dustin with the ability to stand in front of a crowd. He simply exudes that unique combination of business and ministry. So it was our privilege at our annual kick-off meeting shortly after the start of 2024 to recognize him as our first award winner.

There are other recognitions we do each month in our all-employee newsletter and in signage around our Dallas offices—birthdays and work anniversaries are a way to call out people who continue to serve. We recognize employees for referrals, for exceeding goals, for items small and large. Why? Because we understand how important it is to recognize those who serve, especially those who serve unseen.

Informal Recognition

Formal recognition is important, but we should not fail to see the power of informal recognition. This is what Paul does at the close of his letter. He just names a few names, tipping his hat in recognition of some faithful servants. We can do this in the course of every day, at the beginning or the end of almost every gathering. It can and it should be commonplace in our culture.

I saw an executive pastor do this recently. I was the guest preacher sitting on the front row. In his opening greeting, after he welcomed guests, he took ninety seconds to voice appreciation for those who work so hard to keep the grass and landscaping looking good at that church. He called the building superintendent by name and said thank you. How simple is that? I imagine that building superintendent sat a little straighter. Maybe his family was in the service and were able to also recognize their dad's service as unto the Lord. And all it took was less than two minutes of the service to say thanks for a job well done.

When I was in college I was serving as the youth pastor of a small church. A well-known pastor came to speak in our chapel. He was a friend of my parents, but I did not know him well. As he began his message, he said something simple like, "A friend of mine is a student here and doing fine work in a church nearby, seeing several kids come to Christ. It is good to see him here in Chapel. Hance Dilbeck, keep up the good work. I am proud of you."

That was forty years ago, but I can still feel it. He knew me, and he thought what I was doing was significant. He recognized me publicly in detail and called me by name.

For those serving unseen, remember who we serve: the Lord Himself. In Paul's letter to the Colossians, he offers similar sentiments two different ways, both in chapter 3. In verse 17, he says, "And whatever you do, in word or in deed, do everything in the name of the Lord Jesus, giving thanks to God the Father through him." Then, six verses later, after discussing the relationship among families, and slaves and masters, he says, "Whatever you do, do it from the heart, as something done for the Lord and not for people, knowing that you will receive the reward of an inheritance from the Lord. *You serve the Lord Christ*" (vv. 23–24, emphasis mine).

You may feel no one knows your name. You might never have been recognized for your hard work. In fact, you might have been criticized by people who don't understand what goes into your work. Many a media staffer or building maintenance team member have been criticized or even called on the carpet by a leader for something that went wrong. That leader often has no idea of how bad the situation would have been without a Herculean effort on the part of the person in trouble. It's possible you've never received a pat on the back for your work for the kingdom. It's not okay and it shouldn't be acceptable. But please remember: As you serve with excellence, integrity, and skill, the Lord sees; He keeps an account. And He is blessed by your dedication to Him.

Chapter 3

The Psalm

Call to Evening Worship

A song of ascents.

Now bless the LORD,
all you servants of the LORD
who stand in the LORD's house at night!
Lift up your hands in the holy place
and bless the LORD!

May the LORD,
Maker of heaven and earth,
bless you from Zion.
Psalm 134

Serving in the Background

It's hard to visit Arlington National Cemetery in Virginia and not choke up at the sight of the Changing of the Guard. Since April 6, 1948, soldiers from the 3rd U.S. Infantry Regiment, known as "The Old Guard," stand watch over the Tomb of the Unknown Soldier. Their service is done twenty-four hours a day, seven days a week. It's a poignant photograph anytime you see one of these guards standing alone in a blizzard, during hurricane-force winds and rain, not to mention the brutal humid summer heat of the mid-Atlantic. The Sentinels of the Tomb, as the members of The Old Guard are known, are volunteers. They must be in top physical condition, between the height of 5 feet 10 inches and 6 feet 4 inches tall for men or 5 feet 8 inches and 6 feet 2 inches tall for women. To earn the right to serve in any condition around the clock, they must memorize seven pages of the history of Arlington National Cemetery and recite it verbatim.

While the changing of the guards is a ceremony that can be witnessed by the public hourly from October 1 through March 31 or every half hour April 1 through September 30, the public generally can only view it during tour hours,

8:00 a.m. to 5:00 p.m. But the precision, excellence, and commitment to the professionalism and solemness of the task goes on even when the public isn't watching.

Their preparation is done below ground, where they rehearse their history and clean and polish their shoes and weapon. They are meticulous in all they do. The same professionalism, the same regimen, the same commitment is displayed in front of an audience or alone in the dark.

Unseen is not synonymous with *unimportant*. In fact, for the unseen servant, they work without an audience, without applause and without notice. It is vital.

The Hebrew hymn book includes a song for unseen servants. Psalm 134 is a wonderful little song, the last of the Songs of Ascent. These psalms were used to "ascend" to the temple for worship. Jerusalem, sitting atop a hill, would be an ascent for most of those traveling to one of the annual feasts in the Holy City. These psalms helped prepare the pilgrims' heart for worship in the temple. The first, Psalm 120, begins the journey toward Jerusalem from a distant land surrounded by deceitful and divisive people, far away from the temple. The last of the Songs of Ascent, our focus, Psalm 134, puts us in temple at the end of a busy day of worship with the people of God.

When we read this little psalm, we need to remember three things. *First, the song was written to be sung in the temple at night.* This is an after-hours kind of prayer. All the people have gone home; the pilgrims have found a place to rest. The temple was busy and bustling all day long, but now it is quiet. During the day, crowds of people filled the temple. The people saw the priestly leaders dressed in fine robes. They heard the priests sing and pray and teach. They could smell the sacrifices offered in worship. Even the Levites with more humble duties were doing their work in front of hundreds of people, grateful people. But what happened in the temple at night?

The Old Testament teaches us that the Levites were set apart with practical duties that supported the priests in their temple service. Working day and night, the Levites sang, cleaned, stocked, and generally enabled the worship in the temple. They were gatekeepers, burden-bearers, and clean-up crew. Consider this description from 1 Chronicles 23:

> These were the descendants of Levi by their ancestral families—the family heads,

according to their registration by name in the headcount—twenty years old or more, who worked in the service of the LORD's temple. For David said, "The LORD God of Israel has given rest to his people, and he has come to stay in Jerusalem forever. Also, the Levites no longer need to carry the tabernacle or any of the equipment for its service"—for according to the last words of David, the Levites twenty years old or more were to be counted—"but their duty will be to assist the descendants of Aaron with the service of the LORD's temple, being responsible for the courts and the chambers, the purification of all the holy things, and the work of the service of God's temple—as well as the rows of the Bread of the Presence, the fine flour for the grain offering, the wafers of unleavened bread, the baking, the mixing, and all measurements of volume and length. They are also to stand every morning to give thanks and praise to the LORD, and likewise in the evening.

> Whenever burnt offerings are offered to the LORD on the Sabbaths, New Moons, and appointed festivals, they are to offer them regularly in the LORD's presence according to the number prescribed for them. They are to carry out their responsibilities for the tent of meeting, for the holy place, and for their relatives, the descendants of Aaron, in the service of the LORD's temple." (vv. 24–32)

The Levites worked behind the scenes to keep the temple running.

There are a few Levites, however, who serve in the temple after everyone else is asleep. The Old Testament teaches us that some singers were assigned to give thanks to the Lord even in the night. When the people all left for the evening meal and to rest before their journey home, the Lord remained. So David had long ago commanded the Levites to keep on singing. Imagine the soft songs echoing against the stone walls in empty chambers. "Oh give thanks to the LORD for He is good." These Levite singers had an audience of One.

Some Levites worked to clean the temple. People are dirty; on days of holiday festival crowds who had traveled for weeks trampled into the courtyards. These are not angelic beings, but real people. By the end of a busy day the temple might be a messy as an arena after the game, maybe it smelled more like a big barn. Someone had to clean up the mess. As the sun sets, the Levites got to work.

Not only is the temple dirty at the end of the day; the shelves are empty. The utensils used for worship need to be cleaned and set in place for the next day. The ingredients needed for the sacrifices must be replenished. To prepare for the next day of worship, a reset of the building was required.

Some Levites worked security. The gatekeepers had a night shift. These were serving when no one was watching. They carried the keys, kept the watch, protected the sanctity of that holy place so that worship could take place the following morning.

The setting of this psalm reminds me of how a church building feels late Saturday night—quiet, still, empty, sometimes a little creepy, but generally peaceful. It's a unique, spiritual experience to sit in an empty sanctuary on a Saturday night and pray for the next day's service. Few of God's people ever get to experience it, but some make the trip to the building every Saturday evening to make sure things are ready for the next morning. What do they think as they ensure the pews are stocked, check that lights work in the classrooms, refill the bathroom supplies, walk the hallways, clean the doors. Like Harold in our first chapter, they do their work unseen. It is private, privileged, and indispensable service.

Second, by way of background, remember that this psalm was written to be sung antiphonally. It is not only a song to the Lord, but also a song to each other. It moves vertically, between the worshippers and the Lord, but also horizontally, between the worshippers and each other. We find a shift in pronouns between verses 2 and 3. In the first two verses, the leader, maybe a priest, sings to a group, plural, of Levites serving in the temple. In verse 3, the group responds to the singular leader. Thus, the song is sung back and forth.

This movement marks an important biblical truth: worship creates fellowship. When we lift up our hands to the Lord, we will always also stretch out our hand to our brothers and sisters. This is a biblical axiom. Loving God cannot be separated from loving neighbor. Consider what James the brother of Jesus wrote:

> But no one can tame the tongue. It is a restless evil, full of deadly poison. With the tongue we bless our Lord and Father, and with it we curse people who are made in God's likeness. Blessing and cursing come out of the same mouth. My brothers and sisters, these things should not be this way. Does a spring pour out sweet and bitter water from the same opening? (James 3:8–11)

We will return to this truth later in the book.

Finally, to state the obvious, Psalm 134 is short. Depending on the English translation, only around forty words long, twenty-three words in the Hebrew text. Only Psalm 117 is shorter. This brevity brings clarity and promises memory. Since the psalm is so short, we can dig into the details without ever losing sight of the whole.

In the course of reading this book, you ought to consider memorizing this psalm. It would be yours forever, hidden in your heart.

Many people are intimidated by the idea of memorizing Scripture, but Scripture memory is an important spiritual discipline. No doubt, memorizing the forty words of this psalm would bear far more fruit than reading this book about Psalm 134. Scripture memory helps you digest the truth of God's Word.

One of my seminary professors, Dr. Tommy Lea, gave practical wisdom about memorizing Scripture. Note these three important elements in the discipline of Scripture memory.[11]

1. ***Begin with a positive attitude.*** God calls us to hide His Word in our hearts. Every time we think or say that we can't or it's too hard, we doom ourselves to struggle. No matter how old you are or how new Bible study is to you, no matter how much education you have received or how well you read, you CAN memorize Scripture. Why not begin with this short little psalm?
2. ***Memorize the Bible like you eat a meal, one bite at a time.*** Repeat the psalm to the end of the first phrase,

"Behold, bless the Lord." After repeating those four words several times, you have them memorized. Then you can add five more words, "all servants of the Lord." Before you know it, you have half of verse 1 hidden in your heart!

3. ***Review, review, review.*** This is the essence of memorization. Read and say the verse accurately over and over and over again. Memorization involves meditation. Say the verse out loud, even when you are alone. When we are memorizing a verse, we are saying it over and over, day after day. This allows the truth of God's Word to sink deep into our hearts. Like protein is digested to become part of our physical being, so the Word of God is digested to feed our heart, mind, and soul.

Why do I mention Scripture memory in a book on service or unseen servants? Simply because unseen work still plugs into the ultimate work of the local church or ministry, and the gospel is front and center in that work. An unseen servant may not preach God's Word, disciple believers, or lead worship, but servant work is gospel work, and gospel people must know the Scripture!

This little book is written with a desire to unwrap this wonderful psalm and present it as a gift to every unseen servant who reads it. When you memorize the psalm, you carry it with you throughout your work. If you are serving in an unappreciated or unnoticed ministry, if you feel like no one really knows what you do week in and week out, this little psalm is God's gift to you.

Psalm 134:1—Behold

Psalm 134 asks us to pay attention. *NOW*, the Christian Standard Bible says. I also like how the New American Standard Bible captures the start of this psalm: *Behold*. This word is often translated "come" or "look." It is a challenge to see the obvious. It is a sharp command to snap out of our oblivion. The psalm seems to assume that we probably already know what is about to be declared. There is nothing new or obscure in the psalm. No hidden truths waiting to be revealed, just some simple realities that go unrecognized by busy religious workers.

Jesus often used the word *behold*. "*Behold*, the log is in your own eye" (Matt. 7:4 NASB, emphasis mine). "*Behold*, something greater than Solomon is here" (12:42 NASB, emphasis mine). "*Behold*, your house is being left to you desolate" (23:38 NASB, emphasis mine). He often used the word to confront religious people who ought to know better than they seem to know, who have somehow lost their focus.

Sometimes my mother says, "Now, son, you know . . ." when she really means "You ought to know, you used to know, but I am afraid you don't know any longer." It's not quite as jarring as when someone sends a message that starts, "Per my previous email," but it gets the point across! *Behold*, or *come*, calls us back to what we ought to know, draws our attention to some truths we should have been seeing all along—maybe some truths we used to see every day when we went to work, but somehow over the years we have lost sight. Come, behold!

This psalm is a simple call to worship, "Bless the LORD." To bless is to kneel. To bless the Lord is to kneel before the Lord and give Him praise for His unrivaled greatness and

His undeserved goodness. To bless is an act of humility that acknowledges His sufficiency and our insufficiency, His ability and our need.

The psalm repeats the name of the Lord three times in verse 1: the Lord, the Lord, the Lord. Focus, focus, focus. Thus, the psalm is not really about you or me or even the Levites working in the temple. Worship always calls our attention away from ourselves and to the Lord. We want to be like Isaiah in the year that King Uzziah died, "I saw the LORD!" (Isa. 6:1).

Notice who is called to worship.

"Servants of the LORD" is Levitical language. Chronicles calls the Levites who were assigned duties in the tabernacle and later the temple the "servants of the LORD." These Levites were not the priests with special out-front duties. They were not praying public prayers or offering precious sacrifices. These servants were carrying loads, cleaning rooms, and preparing meals, all while staying out of the way, and serving often unnoticed.

Verse 1 says these servants were "serving," literally, "standing" in the house of the Lord. Again, "standing" is biblical vocabulary. It is language that demonstrates these Levites had assigned duties, specific work or responsibilities. They were active, not idle; present, not absent; standing at their post, not derelict in their duties. This is a psalm to faithful, dependable servants.

Even more, the servants in verse 1 are standing at their posts, faithfully fulfilling their duties, even at night. These are not prime-time servants. The House of the Lord could be a crowded place. Some servants of the Lord could and should serve in public, prominent roles. Their duties are fulfilled in front of a packed house of worshippers. But these Levitical servants had the night shift.

Here is the secret sauce of the psalm. This is a song for unseen servants who fulfill their responsibilities even when no one is watching. Some might actually work in a church building or a ministry office after-hours, others work during the day, but far from the spotlight. Unseen servants work in the nursery, on a church van, in a sound booth, behind a desk. If this describes your role, you need to notice one more word in verse 1: "all."

Behold, bless the Lord, *all* servants of the Lord! *All* is a very common word in the Hebrew Testament. We all need to understand the meaning of the word—it means . . . *ALL.*

It includes you, me, our friends, our family, our bosses, and subordinates. It means *ALL.* No servant is excused from the call. No role is left outside the scope of the psalm. All servants, every servant of the Lord is called to worship.

Consider how this verse cuts like a double-edged blade.

On one hand, the psalm calls us to acknowledge people who are serving unseen. It is not insignificant to find that the book of Psalms, the Hebrew hymnbook, includes material that expressly recognizes and includes Levites that might otherwise be overlooked. Without this last of the Psalms of Ascent, these servants might not even enter our thoughts. But the Bible reminds us to acknowledge them, to recognize their work, to show concern for their well-being. This psalm offers the unseen servants a blessing.

Here is an important lesson for every kingdom leader. Recognize the work of the unseen servants in your church or ministry. Who makes sure church happens? Who handles the logistics of ministry? Which people would leave a huge hole no one might know about until they're not there? These are the unseen servants in your ministry.

Pastors should consider this. Walk around and notice the unseen servants. Call them by name, say thank you. Truly see them. After all—these are the people who often help make the pastor look good! Remember your affirmation can help unseen servants feel validated in the work they're called to do for the church.

On the other hand, Psalm 134 reminds every unseen servant of a fundamental truth: We serve an audience of One. It is nice to be seen and appreciated by the people we serve, but that is not our "Why." (In fact, when we take our eyes off the One we serve to look for the approval of men, we likely will grow bitter and resentful.) We began our work with a deep desire to serve the Lord. We must maintain that first love. At the end of the day, we are sustained by one simple truth: the Lord sees our work. Remember, "the Lord, the Lord, the Lord."

When the risen Lord Jesus speaks to the seven churches in John's Revelation, He repeats this reality to each one: "I know your works" (Rev. 2:2, 19; 3:1, 8, 15). Few people in your church or ministry might know what unseen servants do week in and week out. Some may wonder what exactly they do that necessitates their salary and benefits, and occasionally, some ill-tempered member may make comment about it. But rest assured, the Lord knows. And He is blessed by your work.

Behold, bless the Lord, all servants of the Lord, who stand by night in the house of the Lord!

Prayer Point—Verse 1

One of the most powerful things one can do as they read Scripture is to use it as a prayer to grow in their devotional life. The Psalms are a perfect place to hone this discipline. Consider the words in Psalm 134:1:

> Now bless the Lord,
> all you servants of the Lord
> who stand in the Lord's house at night!

Lord, even today I bless You and thank You for the calling You have placed on my life. I thank you for the opportunity to serve You, to serve Your people. You have provided me with the skills, education, aptitude, and talent I need to serve You effectively in this role. Thank You for that. May I bless You in word and in deed. As I serve, may the words out of my mouth and the meditation of my heart be acceptable to You, Lord, my rock and my Redeemer (Ps. 19:14). Amen.

Psalm 134:2—Lift Up Your Hands in the Sanctuary

"Lift up your hands in the holy place and bless the LORD!"

The heart of Psalm 134 is this call to worship: *Bless the Lord!*

Lift up your hands speaks to an intentional commitment to worship. The Bible often speaks about worshippers lifting up their hands to the Lord. Nehemiah describes a dramatic scene when Ezra the scribe calls the people of God back to a right relationship. He stood on a platform to read the Word of God to them. "Ezra opened the book in the sight of all the people for he was standing above all the people; and when he opened it, all the people stood up. Then Ezra blessed the LORD the great God. And all the people answered, 'Amen, Amen!' while lifting up their hands; then they bowed low and worshiped the LORD with their faces to the ground" (Neh. 8:5–6 NASB). Here we see the two primary postures for worship: hands lifted up and face bowed down.

In Lamentations, Jeremiah reminds us of something important. Lifting up our hands is an empty expression unless it reveals a heart of worship. "We lift up our heart and hands toward God in heaven" (Lam. 3:41 NASB). Posture provokes praise, and praise produces posture. We raise our hands because we are raising our hearts to worship the King.

The apostle Paul calls men to a few basic elements of worship. He uses Old Testament language that sounds familiar. "I want the men in every place to pray, lifting up holy hands, without wrath and dissension" (1 Tim. 2:8 NASB). The lifting of hands must never be a ritual disconnected from our lifestyle and our relationships. We love the people around us, we live a life of holiness, and we lift our hands in worship.

The Levites, busy with their work in the night, are called to stop what they are doing and worship. In a sense, much of their work was normal. There isn't much remarkable about cleaning, guarding, and restocking. This was the kind of work being done is homes, shops, and places of business all over Jerusalem. However, their work was in the holy place of the temple.

Notice the movement in verse 2. From heads down and hands full, busy with work, to heads up and hands raised in worship.

Unseen servants must be careful to worship while we work.

The old Scottish preacher Alexander MacLaren once said while preaching from Psalm 134, "The more diligently our hands and thoughts are employed about the externals of religious duties, the more we must see to it that our inmost spirits are baptized into fellowship with God."[12] Here is one of the subtle risks for religious workers.

Imagine someone working for a missionary-sending organization who long ago stopped praying for the salvation of the nations. He might be a talented employee; he might have been recognized for his work. He employs best practices, brings breakfast from time to time, and is a joy to be around. But he's lost the wonder of the calling on his life.

Or imagine someone vacuuming a worship center without ever worshipping. He grimaces every time it rains, knowing someone is going to track mud on *his* carpet that *he* has worked dutifully to clean.

Imagine processing the financial gifts of contributors without ever giving thanks for God's provision. She grumbles over the wads of folded-up money or the loose change in an offering plate. God's providing for His kingdom's work—of which she is a part—yet she fails to see the awe and majesty of it all.

There's an old preacher story of an architect coming upon a beautiful house of worship he had designed and encountered three bricklayers. He asks the first one what he's doing, and he replies, "I'm building a wall." The architect moves on to the second bricklayer and asks the same question, to which this bricklayer says, "I'm helping to build this church building." Finally, the architect approaches the third bricklayer and asks the same question, to which this bricklayer answers, "I'm building a cathedral to the glory of Almighty God."

One of these behind-the-scenes workers understood the worship that goes with his service.

It is possible to work in a holy place, a place set apart for worship and ministry, while totally neglecting the Holy One. It is possible for someone to work at a kingdom ministry, while neglecting the King Himself.

Our little psalm builds an intentional hedge against the hypocrisy of worship-less work for a religious worker.

I consider myself a sort of a Levite. Most of my life, I served as the pastor of a local church. Much of what I did was public, the connection of my work to the church was obvious. I stood on the platform proclaiming Scripture in sermons week in and week out. I led staff meetings, baptized new believers, distributed the elements for the Lord's Supper. Everyone in the church knew me.

Now, as president of GuideStone, I serve the kingdom in a different way. My work is a few steps removed from the local church. I am the leader of a large number of employees and often spend my days making administrative leadership decisions. It's easy as an unseen servant to slip into the pattern of head down, hands busy, but heart far from the One we serve. How do I ensure that doesn't happen? I brought my prayer bench with me. I moved my kneeling bench from my pastor's office to my president's office. That piece of furniture reminds me to worship while I work. I stop at regular times in my workday to kneel on that bench, to raise up my head and my hands to the Lord. I bless Him with praise and seek His blessing as I worship Him.

Might I suggest taking time each day to focus on Him? Praise Him. Worship Him. Ask Him for His favor and direction. Give Him the glory.

Like the Levites who worked in the temple at night, we are called to worship while we work. In fact, this little psalm is a call to worship.

Consider how this psalm teaches us to incorporate the discipline of worship into our workday using time, place, and posture. Incorporate set times of worship into your daily or weekly routine. It does not need to be long. It should not take away from your productivity. Just a beep on your watch or ten minutes on your calendar that call you to stop your work and bless the Lord.

What about a special place of worship like my prayer bench? A room in the building or a piece of furniture that calls us to worship every time we pass by. Sit on the playground and pray for the children who will play there, sit on the front pew and praise the Holy One, kneel in a prayer room and ask for the Lord's help. Find places of worship in your place of work.

Posture matters. Sure, we can worship while we walk down a hallway and pray while our hands are busy. However, Psalm 134 reminds us of the power of posture. Stop your movement, lift up your hands, bow your head, kneel in His presence, and worship.

To be clear, everyone ought to worship while they work. Every Christ-follower ought to be worshipping the Lord no matter where they work or what they do. However, those who labor behind the scenes in a church or ministry must exercise a special degree of discipline. A pattern of worship will protect us from the subtle risk of our work. Blessing hedges against bitterness.

Prayer Point—Verse 2

Verse 2 gives us an interesting insight. Our workplace is a holy place, set aside for the work He has called us to. Take time to pray for work.

> Lift up your hands in the holy place
> and bless the Lord!

Lord, as I focus on You in this pause from work, surrounded by the tools of my calling, I confess that this is Holy Ground; Lord, help me to treat it as such. You are the reason I have this role; I serve You, my audience of One. Thank You for this place and may we use all of it for Your glory and our good. Amen.

Psalm 134:3—May the LORD Bless You

In the final verse the Levites respond to the call to worship from the leader. Consider how this psalm functions in the temple. At a set time in the night shift of the temple service, a priestly leader calls out these words with a voice loud and clear.

We learn several important lessons about kingdom service from verse 3 of this little psalm.

First, God's blessing flows from Zion to all of earth and the heavens. In his commentary on Psalms, Derek Kidner reminds us that "Zion [is] a particular and discoverable place."[13] Yet from this particular place the Lord God, who created heaven and earth, has chosen to bless people. His blessing flows from the particular to all creation.

In the New Testament, Zion is associated with Calvary. From the cross of Jesus flows the blessing of God. Remember Hebrews 12:

> For you have not come to what could be touched, to a blazing fire, to darkness, gloom, and storm, to the blast of a trumpet, and the sound of words. Those who heard it begged

> that not another word be spoken to them, for they could not bear what was commanded: "If even an animal touches the mountain, it must be stoned." The appearance was so terrifying that Moses said, "I am trembling with fear." Instead, you have come to Mount Zion, to the city of the living God (the heavenly Jerusalem), to myriads of angels, a festive gathering, to the assembly of the firstborn whose names have been written in heaven, to a Judge, who is God of all, to the spirits of righteous people made perfect, and to Jesus, the mediator of a new covenant, and to the sprinkled blood, which says better things than the blood of Abel. (vv. 18–24)

When Psalm 134 sings of the Lord blessing people from Zion, followers of Jesus Christ should ponder how God's blessing flows from the finished work of Jesus on the cross. The One who made heaven and earth intervened to redeem all creation at the cross. In Him, we have redemption. Through His blood, we are forgiven of our trespasses according to the riches of His grace. The Lord blesses us from Zion.

Zion is a reference to Jerusalem, to the temple. The temple is the place of sacrifice or propitiation. Jesus shed His blood as the atoning sacrifice for our sins.

> My little children, I am writing you these things so that you may not sin. But if anyone does sin, we have an advocate with the Father—Jesus Christ the righteous one. He himself is the atoning sacrifice for our sins, and not only for ours, but also for those of the whole world. (1 John 2:1–2)

Indeed, the Lord does bless us from Zion!

Psalm 2 is one of the most important of all Old Testament psalms. It is a Messianic psalm often used as the sermon text for the apostles. In Psalm 2, the Lord says,

> "But as for Me, I have installed My King
> Upon Zion, My holy mountain." (v. 6 NASB)

Zion is where Jesus Christ sits enthroned. He died on the cross to reverse the curse and bring us blessings of redemption and grace. It is from Zion that we seek and find the Lord's blessing.

Second, faithful servants return blessings to leaders. Like the Levites on the night shift, unseen servants today often serve under the leadership of others. When we hear the call of the leader, how do we respond? Do we grumble, groan, resist, or resent the leader? Are we critical of his manner or tone or direction? It is easy to develop a bad attitude toward the leaders. One of the challenges of ministry, especially those who get called from the pew to the staff, is they see their leaders for the flawed human beings they are. It's easy to put your best face on Sunday morning for a couple of hours; it's much harder to do that during office hours Monday through Friday! Leaders are so often unaware of our challenges, disconnected from the realities of our tasks.

In Psalm 134, the Levites respond to the exhortation of the leader with benediction: "May the Lord bless you"! How this seasons the corridors of the temple with grace!

A healthy relationship between Christian leaders and workers is a vital kingdom distinctive. We recall that the people of God have always tended to grumble and complain about the leader. The Bible word is "murmur." Murmuring against the leader is as old as Moses. And it always keeps the people from moving forward.

The book of Acts tells us that this same kind of complaining threatened the early church in Jerusalem. "Now at this time while the disciples were increasing in number, a complaint arose . . ." (Acts 6:1 NASB). This kind of grumbling can keep a church or ministry from fulfilling its mission. The Bible challenges us to support leaders so they can fulfill their calling without grief (Heb. 13:17). That word *grief* means "to groan." It describes a feeling which is internal and unexpressed.

We want to strive to be such a blessing for our boss that he will not groan when he sees us coming down the hallway. We want to be a blessing, not a burden.

When there is grace exchanged between followers and leaders in a ministry workplace, when the direction and exhortation of a leader receives support and blessing, the whole ministry is lifted, and the Lord is pleased. On the other hand, bitterness can creep in to poison the relationships between leaders and team. When the unseen servants are pronouncing the Lord's blessing on leaders, the people of God are encouraged and the Lord Himself is blessed. The call to worship creates fellowship between the leader and the team.

Finally, let's take time to consider the way the psalm uses the word *bless*. We bless the Lord, and the Lord blesses us. The unseen servants are called to worship and bless the Lord, and the leader calls on the Lord to bless the servants. *Bless*. The vocabulary does not change. The same word is used three times: bless, bless, bless. But surely the meaning of the word shifts.

When we lift up our hands and bless the Lord with our glad submission and praise, we must be doing something different than when the Lord moves in faithfulness and grace to bless us. How does this crucial biblical vocabulary function?

Again, Kidner sums it up well: "The word *bless* is perhaps the key-note of the psalm, sounded as it is in each verse. So far, it has been directed Godward; now it returns from God to man. But the exchange is quite unequal: to bless God is to acknowledge gratefully what he is; but to bless man, God must make of him what he is not, and give him what he has not."[14]

This little psalm reveals the unequal exchange that is the heart of the gospel. We serve the Lord because He alone deserves our devotion. We praise the Lord because He alone deserves our praise. We ascribe to the Lord the glory due His name for He alone is worthy. He deserves everything we offer to Him and more. Yet, the exchange is unequal.

He calls us His children, not His slaves. When we are faithless, He remains faithful. He embraces us, enrobes us, celebrates our repentance when we deserve to be forever away, ashamed, and on the outside. In short, He gives us what we don't deserve, a blessing. He gives us grace.

We bless the Lord, and the Lord blesses us; but the exchange is far from equal.

Prayer Point—Verse 3

Verse 3 offers a call to one another. Those workers that sometimes give us grief or indigestion, they are co-laborers in the gospel and in the work of His kingdom, which is without end.

> May the LORD,
> Maker of heaven and earth,
> bless you from Zion.

Father, thank You for the men and women with whom I serve. We are humans and we have times of discouragement toward one another. But Lord, let those times be few. Bless them in the work of their hands. Bless them as they seek to serve You. Bless them as they have families and pressures of their own. Allow us all to be a team for Your glory. Amen.

Chapter 4

How to Serve Well, Unseen

Call to Evening Worship

A song of ascents.

Now bless the Lord,
all you servants of the Lord
who stand in the Lord's house at night!
Lift up your hands in the holy place
and bless the Lord!

May the Lord,
Maker of heaven and earth,
bless you from Zion.
Psalm 134

Most traffic accidents occur close to home. In fact, one study published by the National Institutes of Health found that among 3,280 patients (2005–2010), 88 percent were injured within ten miles of home.[15] Wow! Several factors contribute to this reality, but one should be considered here. When we get close to home, we get comfortable, and we drop our guard. Carelessness causes crashes.

As we observed earlier, those who serve behind the scenes in a church or a Christian ministry work in a high-risk zone. Unseen servants are not vulnerable in the same ways to the pitfalls of the "platform" servants—sins like pride, greed, and entitlement. But they are exposed to some subtle, but serious, risks. Psalm 134 helps us to consider these subtle dangers and build hedges to protect us.

What to Watch Out for in Unseen Service

Guard Your Heart Against Bitterness: Embrace Unseen Service

When we serve unseen, we are often unappreciated. Thoughts may come up like, *My pastor would never notice my work unless I messed something up,* or *Our executive director has no idea of my name.* When people take our work for granted, it is easy to develop a bit of resentment. Ironically, when one is committed to her work, she is more exposed to bitterness. Week after week of delivering at a high standard without recognition can harden the heart. We grow sarcastic and cynical. No one accepts a role of unseen service out of a desire to be praised. However, being overlooked is a bitter pill to swallow.

Bitterness is an interesting word. It is one of four basic taste sensations: sweet, sour, salty, and bitter. Bitterness describes a taste; and we use the word to describe a feeling that lurks deep down inside. It is a feeling of resentment that breeds hostility. Bitterness is toxic.

The Word of God warns us of how bitterness can hide for years in the deep parts of our being, shrouded from the people around us. "The heart knows its own bitterness" (Prov. 14:10). The New Testament also speaks to the deep-down nature of bitterness. The book of Hebrews speaks of the "root of bitterness." What a powerful word picture. "See to it that no one comes short of the grace of God; that no root of bitterness springing up causes trouble, and by it many be defiled" (Heb. 12:15 NASB). "Root of bitterness speaks to the two aspects of bitterness. It is hidden, but at some point it comes to the surface."

Roots are hidden beneath the soil. They cannot be seen until they spring up. Roots bear shoots and fruit. We cannot know when or how, but this is what roots do. The Bible speaks of the "root of bitterness" to warn us that the bitterness we hold onto deep within will spring to the surface in unexpected ways, impacting our lives.

Paul helps us anticipate how the root of bitterness often comes to the surface:

> Let no unwholesome word proceed from your mouth, but only such a word as is good for edification according to the need of the moment, so that it will give grace to those who hear. Do not grieve the Holy Spirit of God, by whom you were sealed for the day of redemption. Let all bitterness and wrath and anger and clamor and slander be put away from you, along with all malice. (Eph. 4:29–31 NASB)

Notice the connection between the bitterness hiding in the heart and the words that spring from our mouths. Words are often the fruit that spring from the root of bitterness. Eventually, the ugliness of the heart finds expression. Maybe your bitterness is not as hidden as you think.

Jesus taught us that our mouths speak out what fills our hearts. What does your daily conversation reveal about the condition of your heart? If you could rewind and replay everything you said yesterday, what would you hear? Are you overly critical, finding fault, quick to complain. Would you find a certain bitterness if you really took time to taste your words?

So how can we protect ourselves from this bitterness that can creep in? Thankfully, the psalmist gives us an answer.

Psalm 134 leads us to *embrace unseen service.* The psalm elevates the status of those servants of the Lord who stand at their post at night. The Bible assigns a particular dignity to those who fulfill their God-given duties unseen.

Unseen service is countercultural. We are living in the day of "selfies." Most people seem to be infected with the notion that what we are doing doesn't really matter unless it is heralded publicly and "liked."

According to NIH researchers, the main reasons encouraging people to post their photos online are "the desire to increase their self-esteem; communication; transfer and preservation of information; entertainment; or seeking self-approval, maintaining a sense of belonging and preserve one's memories and experiences."[16]

What is not recognized is deemed unreal in our day and time.

The timeless biblical message, however, is different. To work unseen does not diminish our work; in fact, it actually elevates it. Consider the teaching of Jesus. He warned His disciples against praying or giving or fasting to be seen. He called those who serve to be seen hypocrites, and warns: "Truly I tell you, they have their reward" (Matt. 6:2).

On the other hand, He has a special promise for those who serve unseen. When people fail to see our faithfulness, our Father is watching. When people fail to recognize or reward our work, the Father will not fail: "Your Father who sees in secret will reward you" (v. 4). What a promise! Christian servants embrace unseen service as a special opportunity to please the Father.

Jesus condemned the religious leaders who always pressed to sit in the seats of honor, up front, in the spotlight. He commends those unseen servants who are willing to sit at the back of the room or stand in the kitchen. It's wise to wait for the Master to call us up front.

It could be that the Lord has gifted a person for unseen service, or maybe this is a season of his or her life. Later, in some other season of service, that same person might be up front or on the platform. "Humble yourselves, therefore, under the mighty hand of God, so that he may exalt you at the proper time, casting all your cares on him, because he cares about you" (1 Pet. 5:6–7). The point is, if you are at the end of the table, in the back of the room, out of the spotlight, the Lord sees you.

We recently installed a security doorbell at my house. To be honest, I spend too much time watching the video. I have seen squirrels, raccoons, even a bobcat. I am fascinated by the people that come to the front door. Some seem to be very aware that the unblinking doorbell is watching, but most seem to be too busy to notice.

Recently, a delivery person rang the doorbell when we were away. While she waited, some sort of flying insect attacked her. She began swatting and twisting and screaming. Soon, she successfully ended the life of what I assume was a wasp. Then she did something impressive.

She cleaned up the mess. She had no interest in touching the smashed critter, but she pulled a piece of paper from her pocket and carefully removed it from my porch. She threw the dead wasp into our shrubs. She did not want the homeowner to come home to a smashed bug.

The fact that she cleaned up the mess when no one was watching makes it more impressive. I appreciated it more. Your Father is watching. If you serve faithfully when no one is noticing, it is even more impressive to the Lord. Trust Him to reward you.

We can embrace unseen service because we believe that our Father is watching. One day, He will recognize us for our faithfulness. This truth sets us free from the bitterness that would rob us of our joy. It gives us the pleasure of serving unseen with a smile on our face.

Psalm 134 teaches us to embrace unseen service and reject bitterness. And there's more.

Guard Your Hearts Against Coldness: Worship While You Work

We discussed this a bit in the previous chapter, but it bears repeating here: Unseen servants must also guard their hearts against coldness. Too often, those who work behind the scenes in ministry develop a cold hard heart toward worship. Paul admonishes that we are to present ourselves as "a living and holy sacrifice, acceptable to God, which is [our] spiritual service of worship" (Rom. 12:1 NASB). We must guard against coldness of heart; our service must be one of worship. As discussed in the previous chapter, Psalm 134 models a pattern of worship for those who are serving in the Lord's house at night. The psalm provides the Levites a moment, a manner, and a model for worship. It is not enough for us to have our hands full and our heads down in work. We must stop, lift up our hands, and bless the Lord.

Worship hedges against the cold heart that can creep in for the unseen servant.

For years, my sister lived on a mountainside just outside of Pagosa Springs, Colorado. She and my brother-in-law had a wonderful piece of land. The view out their front door was breathtaking—a lush valley with cattle grazing, tall pines in the foreground and in the distance and across the valley were mountain peaks soaring to 14,000 feet. The clouds, the light, the view—all were constantly changing, and they were always magnificent.

When I visited from time to time, I couldn't stop gazing at the beauty. It was so captivating. But they lived there 365 days a year and they had work to do. They were doing their jobs, fulfilling responsibilities, keeping schedules. They walked in and out of the house with heads down and hands full. But, from time to time, they stopped to behold the beauty.

From time to time, in the midst of days full of work, the unseen servant must stop to behold the beauty of the Lord. Worship while you work. If we work in close proximity to the "things of the Lord" without lifting our hands, our heads, and our hearts to the Lord, we will grow cold. Our hearts will be hard, and we will lose our sensitivity to the Spirit's call to worship.

Marva Dawn has said "Worship is our glad response to the immense grace of the triune God."[17] In worship, we respond to who God is and to all He has done for us through Jesus. Worship brings perspective. Worship brings the proper perspective to our world, our lives, and our service. Without worship, we will lose perspective.

David understood the power of perspective that comes through worship. Psalm 27 speaks of a season of life marked by fear, adversaries, and trouble. Yet, David remains confident. The key is the proper perspective gained in worship. "I have asked one thing from the LORD; it is what I desire: to dwell in the house of the LORD all the days of my life, gazing on the beauty of the LORD and to seeking him in his temple" (Ps. 27:4).

When the unseen servant stops worshipping, he loses sight of his calling. Gratitude is replaced with grumbling. Though, in a sense, he is working in "the house of the LORD," a distance develops. The Lord's worth is minimized, and our own worth is exaggerated. The work of the servant matters, so always guard against the coldness of worship-less work.

Years ago, I served as the pastor of a fine church with a staff of a few dozen people. One of our custodial staff was an older gentleman. He loved the Lord. We were in the midst of Vacation Bible School (VBS). You may have never considered this, but Vacation Bible School is like D-Day for a church custodian. Talk about disruption!

During VBS the calm order of a weekly routine turns to chaos. Teachers come early and stay late. They decorate walls, move furniture, adjust thermostats—often as their own children run wild through the hallways. Then the rest of the children show up.

Boys and girls from four to fourteen fill the building. Rooms built for children are full to overflowing, while rooms not built for children are rearranged for that purpose. Imagine the tracked-in mud, chairs marking floors, trash cans overflowing, cookie crumbs, and Kool-Aid stains. You get the picture—some of you may have shuddered at the thought! It is enough to put a custodian over the edge. But our custodian seemed to embrace it all in stride.

Midway through VBS week, I noticed something remarkable. The children were gathered for a closing assembly. They were practicing for a presentation they would make for their parents at the end of the week. Standing at the back of the room was our custodian, mop in hand. Guess what he was doing. He was singing along! As the children sang a simple song of praise, he joined in worship. Worship the Lord while you work and your heart will stay warm and tender.

If your ministry has a chapel service, worship with your coworkers. Don't just show up and go through the motions; sing, pray, participate. If you are mopping the floor under the pews, sit down and meditate in the quiet. Cast your cares upon the Lord while you enjoy the silence. If you hear the children in the nursery singing, sing along. When your team prays before staff meeting, bless the Lord in your prayer. If you have a break in the midst of the busy day, use the prayer room. Worship while you work.

Don't Be Cranky: Bless the People Around You

That's a great word, isn't it: *cranky*; ill-tempered, grouchy, cross. We have all encountered far too many religious workers who somehow over their years of service grew cranky. We all remember the church secretary who intimidated the young ministers, or the custodian who resented anyone who dared to use the building, or the nursery worker who made you feel guilty for bringing your kids to church. No one seeks employment in a church or ministry with the intent to become an irritable grouch, but far too many do just that.

Psalm 134 reminds us that the vertical and the horizontal are connected. When we are living and working to bless the Lord, we will also bless those around us. We will bless our coworkers, our leaders, and the people we serve. "May the LORD bless." We want to live and serve in such a way as to be a blessing for people. After all, "blessed people bless people."

Here is a warning sign to protect us from this subtle pitfall. If we are doing the Lord's work but don't like the Lord's people, watch out! Read those words again. The moment that you lose sight of the fact the Lord's work *is* the Lord's people, you're on very dangerous ground.

This is not a novel truth. It is bedrock Christianity. Remember that Jesus was asked to declare the most important commandment. He refused to name just one, but two.

> He said to him, "'Love the Lord your God with all your heart, with all your soul, and with all your mind.' This is the greatest and most important command. The second is like it: 'Love your neighbor as yourself.' All the Law and the Prophets depend on these two commands." (Matt. 22:37–40)

You want to live so as to be a blessing to the people you serve, the people you serve with, and the people you serve under. Sometimes, the very people we set out to serve become a burden to us. I heard a pastor once say, half-jokingly, "This would be a good job if it wasn't for these people." Whether working behind the scenes in a local church or a large ministry, if we are not careful a subtle shift will distort our work. We will begin to serve the ministry, not the people. We will focus on calendars, buildings, programs, budgets, and view the people as a source of disruption and frustration. But our purpose is to serve these people.

Remember that Jesus consistently had to remind the religious types of His day that their systems and buildings and routines and rules were made for the people, not the other way around. For example, one Sabbath day the disciples were hungry. As they walked through a grain field, they picked heads of grain to eat. The Pharisees complained that they were breaking the Sabbath rules by picking the grain. Jesus would have none of it.

He confronted the Pharisees for viewing people with disregard. He said, "The Sabbath was made for man and not man for the Sabbath" (Mark 2:27). We must maintain a mindset of servanthood. Our churches and ministries exist to serve people in the name of Christ. Are you blessing the people you serve? With your words, your deeds, and your disposition, do you bless them?

We are also called to *bless the people around us.* How is it to be around you at work? Are you kind? Cooperative? What is the tone of your conversation? Do you think other people enjoy working with you? Do you bless them?

When we walked through Paul's list of unseen servants in Romans 16, you might have noticed a repeated word: fellow workers. When Paul writes about his work for the Lord, he is consistently mindful of the people working with him—co-laborers, fellow workers. In fact, Paul uses that word a dozen times in his letters. We should share this biblical perspective.

The Lord has placed you in your ministry to bless the people who serve alongside you. At times, we can be so determined to excel in our work that we neglect our coworkers. If we have a sour disposition toward the people who serve alongside us, this is a clear indicator we have lost a Christ-honoring posture toward our service.

Bless the people you serve and bless the people you serve alongside.

It is always easy to develop a bad attitude toward one's boss. Bosses can be blind. Bosses have faults of their own. Bosses can fail to appreciate unseen servants. However, if we are to keep our heart right in ministry, we must keep our heart right with our supervisors. Give them some grace.

The health of every church and ministry depends on healthy working relationships within the staff. Whether your staff is comprised of three or three hundred, love, encourage, appreciate, and support one another. People who tolerate a bad attitude toward their supervisor are falling prey to one of the most subtle pitfalls of the work. This can be an infection that spreads throughout the entire church or ministry. Guard your relationship with whomever you work with.

Unseen servants should pray for your boss. Encourage your boss. Cooperate with them in every aspect of the work. Determine to be a source of joy and peace, not a burden to bear.

It is possible for an unseen servant to find his good work spoiled by bad relationships. As you work, bless the people around you.

Thomas Watson died in 1686. He was a Cambridge-educated pastor and scholar but found himself ejected from his pulpit by the Act of Conformity in 1662. He was a well-known preacher, and Charles Spurgeon said his fame was "well-deserved." He wrote a book about Christian character. The book has one of those great, very descriptive, Puritan titles, *The Godly Man's Picture: Drawn with a Scripture Pencil.* In the book, Watson uses the Bible to present some fundamental characteristics of a man who is going to heaven. One important section of the book is titled "A Godly Man Is Good in His Relationships." "To call one who is bad in his relationships godly, is a contradiction; it is to call evil good (Isaiah 5:20). . . . Not to be good in our relationships spoils all our other good things."[18]

What Watson writes is not a deep mystery. It is not profound because no one ever considered it. No, the power comes from the fact that he speaks of such a plain Bible principle. Yet it is a principle so often overlooked by unseen servants. "To call one who is bad in his relationships godly, is a contradiction; it is to call evil good. . . . Not to be good in our relationships spoils all our other good things." Every unseen servant must protect her relationships. To be a good servant, to be a good Christian, is to maintain good relationships with those we serve, those we serve with, and those we serve under.

Every servant of Christ ought to seek to be like Philemon. Consider what Paul wrote to this faithful servant.

> For I have great joy and encouragement from your love, because the hearts of the saints have been refreshed through you, brother. (Philem. 7)

That word *refreshed* paints a beautiful picture. The word means to give an intermission from labor, to give a rest. It describes taking a break in the midst of your work. Imagine a farmer in the field on a hot day, finally finding some shade, sitting down in the soft grass, taking off his hat to wipe his brow, and drinking a cup of cool water. Refreshed.

Jesus used this great word when He invited weary sinners to come find salvation: "Come to me, all of who are weary and burdened, and I will give you *rest*" (Matt. 11:28, emphasis mine).

Consider this remarkable reality. We can give rest to the people around us at work. With our words, through our help, even with our attitude, we can provide a bit of cool shade in the midst of a stressful day. Unseen servant, if you give rest to the people around you, you are doing it right. It is possible to serve Christ in such a way that you can lighten their load, give them rest and peace; in short, you can bless the people you work with.

Working behind the scenes in a church or Christian ministry is rewarding and risky. We can hedge against the common and subtle pitfalls if we embrace unseen service, worship while we work, and always bless the people around us.

Chapter 5

A Special Case of the Seen Unseen: The Pastor's Wife

Call to Evening Worship

A song of ascents.

Now bless the LORD,
all you servants of the LORD
who stand in the LORD's house at night!
Lift up your hands in the holy place
and bless the LORD!

May the LORD,
Maker of heaven and earth,
bless you from Zion.
Psalm 134

Perhaps no one is more unseen than the pastor's wife. That may be odd to say, since she likely serves in every way around the church, from hosting baby showers to bringing meals to Bible study teacher to choir member to being the pastor's unofficial secretary. But it's often a thankless job, one that is assumed—more than one church has considered the pastor and his wife a two-people-for-the-price-of-one calling—and one that too often isn't considered. The pastor's wife is very visible but often unappreciated, taken for granted.

One of the hallmarks of serving unseen is that if you're doing your job well, people don't notice. The moment there is a mistake, or the moment you take a day off, or your position is unfilled, everyone notices. That is incredibly true for the pastor's wife.

The pastor's wife often knows everything that is going on. She is expected to be the perfect wife, mother, confidante, host, and more. It can be trying. In 2017, Lifeway Research conducted its Survey of American Pastors' Spouses.[19] In the survey of 722 spouses from across Protestant denominations, it was generally good news, with 90 percent reporting that they thought "ministry has had a positive effect on their family" and 85 percent saying, "The church we serve takes good care of us."

There were challenges though—68 percent worry about financial matters, including saving enough for retirement, and half saying they "feel they live in a fishbowl."

Serving as a pastor's wife is one of the most unique unseen roles, because while she is often in front of the church, faithful in supporting her husband, she is not given full credit for her work. Her church job is unpaid, yet everyone has an opinion of her work and how well she is doing. Instead of one annual review that many employees receive, she gets weekly reviews in the minds of members, and sometimes they are shared with her whether valid or not, whether fair or not, whether charitable or not. In the same Lifeway survey, 69 percent report that they don't have many (or any) close confidantes in the church.

That can lead to burnout and other frustrations. Lifeway reports that on a scale of 0 to 6—with 0 being not at all, and 6 being every day—22 percent score a 4, 5, or 6 to the statement, "I feel burned out from my work as a minister's spouse." A slightly smaller percentage score the same on the "I have become more callous toward people since my spouse took this job." Half report "experiencing personal attacks in their current church."

Over a lifetime of church service, I've learned every field of service, secular or sacred, has its own challenges. Ministry has its unique challenges, though, that aren't always understood by those outside. The pastor's wife serves in a role unlike any other. She knows pressures and demands that most people cannot imagine. She lives in a complex tapestry of relationships that is off the charts! She fulfills a role that impacts a church in a significant way, but few people realize it.

The marriage relationship of pastor and wife is vital. Most couples understand this and invest in their marriage. Wise pastors understand that "house and wealth are inherited from fathers, but a prudent wife is from the Lord" (Prov. 19:14). Both husband and wife value their marriage and invest in one another. Husbands love their wives and wives support their husbands in life and service.

But the fact that your husband loves you doesn't mean you can ignore your own resilience. As a special kind of unseen servant, you must be careful to hedge against the hypocrisy that can creep into your week. What I share in previous chapters applies to you.

Embrace Unseen Service

Every pastor's wife must serve with confidence that the Father sees. The Father knows every detail of your work. He sees what is said, what is done, what goes unsaid or unacknowledged. Even when it seems that most people fail to notice your faithfulness, the Father sees. He knows your deeds. He will reward you in due season.

Many pastors' wives knew generally what they were getting themselves into when they got married. You came from a pastor's household, or had strong mentors in premarriage counseling, or you found a strong mentor during your husband's seminary training. That doesn't make the path you're on easier (nor should it be used as a verbal cudgel to tell you to "get over it" when the stress eats at you), it merely acknowledges you understood that the road would be difficult.

Some, though, find themselves called to be a pastor's wife well after marriage, maybe even after your husband was established in a career. Marcos Urbina[20] was a church planter in California. Growing up a pastor's son in rural Mexico, Marcos originally did not believe ministry was a call for him. After a severe famine, which took two brothers' lives, he moved to the United States and took a job in the aviation industry at a manufacturing plant in California. He began volunteering in the music ministry at the First Baptist Church of Los Angeles when God called him to the ministry. Despite making what he described as "good money," and watching his father suffer for meager pay in Mexico, he surrendered to the call and began pastoring and planting a church. The little church he and his wife, Esther, started grew quickly, ultimately becoming the second-largest Mexican Baptist church in California.

Esther was alongside him for more than sixty years, originally marrying an immigrant to America with a stable job, and ended up a pastor's wife, a role she embraced.

It can be easy to resent that call if you're not careful, but it's important to remember that God will equip those He calls; He doesn't necessarily call the qualified.

When I was beginning my life as a pastor, an old preacher challenged me to know the value of my committed godly wife. After paying her some wonderful compliments, he turned to me with this truth: "Your wife can't make you a good pastor, but she could sure keep you from being one." Over thirty years later, I would agree.

The pastor's wife plays an essential, but unappreciated role. She must believe her service is seen by the Father.

Create a Habit of Worship and Time Alone with God

Public worship can be a challenge for the pastor's wife. There is so much bouncing around your brain on Sunday morning. All the normal distractions abound, like attending to volunteer responsibilities, making sure your children are in place, greeting your friends. On top of that, if you are not careful, you might carry the burden of concern to the entire operation.

Too often the pastor's wife sits through the worship service focusing on 101 issues other than the glory of God. *Is the temperature too hot in the room? Is the music too loud? Did I properly greet the new family? Oh, I wish my husband had chosen a better set of words!*

Hear the Master say, "Martha, Martha, you are worried and bothered about so many things; but only one thing is necessary" (Luke 10:41–42 NASB). Like everyone else who is working during the worship time, the pastor's wife must protect some time for corporate worship. To pray undistracted, to praise uninhibited, to listen with an undivided heart as she gives her full focus to the One.

Worship-less work makes one weary.

The good news in 2017 was Lifeway found slightly more than half "had personal time with the Lord involving Bible study and prayer five or more times" in the previous week. The bad news? A quarter had two or fewer times alone with the Lord. That is not sustainable if you're seeking to follow the Lord. Find time to get alone with Him to pray and to grow in your own spiritual walk. You can't survive in this vital role if you don't have time alone with the Lord.

I certainly don't want to add to what is often a taxing schedule. Perhaps the best way to add some prayer time is to listen to Scripture in the car as you run errands or between appointments. Windshield time can make for good prayer time, as can listening to worship music. Some of us, whether in church leadership, church membership, in seen or unseen ministries, who find we "don't have time for a quiet time," might find a lot more time available if we give up doom-scrolling or jumping into every denominational or political fight that erupts on social media. Worship is not an option for any Christian; serving unseen or marrying a pastor doesn't exempt one from that command.

Bless the People You Work With

Remember, the vertical and the horizontal are connected. When we are living and working to bless the Lord, we will also bless those around us. This can be difficult. After all, people may share unflattering views with you of your husband or have critiques on how you raise your children. They may also not pay your husband what he's worth. Criticism that cuts can come to the pastor's wife.

Every pastor's wife must maintain a posture ready to bless others. Paul's counsel to the church at Rome might help.

> Bless those who persecute you; bless and do not curse. Rejoice with those who rejoice; weep with those who weep. Live in harmony with one another. Do not be proud; instead, associate with the humble. Do not be wise in your own estimation. Do not repay anyone evil for evil. Give careful thought to do what

> is honorable in everyone's eyes. If possible, as far as it depends on you, live at peace with everyone. Friends, do not avenge yourselves; instead, leave room for God's wrath, because it is written, "Vengeance belongs to me; I will repay," says the Lord. But "If your enemy is hungry, feed him. If he is thirsty, give him something to drink. For in so doing you will be heaping fiery coals on his head." Do not be conquered by evil, but conquer evil with good. (Rom. 12:14–21)

The unseen servant can be a force for peace and a force for good by refusing to react to negative criticism, or "curses"; instead, choosing to extend a blessing to the people with whom we serve and worship. The pastor's wife can be a thermostat, not a thermometer, as she helps set the spiritual climate—instead of simply recoding it. She can, often in a quiet off-the-radar way, be a kind of baffle in the tank that settles the waves that come to every fellowship.

Many pastors' wives fail to appreciate the power of their words. Whether written or spoken, a word of kindness or appreciation from the pastor's wife carries weight. Her words can build up or tear down. Her words can fan the flames of a church fight or put out the fire before it spreads. If you watch your words, you will make your way with people. Determine to be a blessing.

A Word about Finances

In a 2017 Lifeway survey, 61 percent of spouses indicated that "Our family's financial situation requires more than the salary received from the church."[21] That is unsurprising for those of us who serve at GuideStone. Research we conducted in 2022 along with Lifeway and Baptist state conventions showed pastors' salaries—already low and negatively impacted by shrinking budgets in the wake of the COVID-19 pandemic—have failed to keep pace with inflation. The historic period of inflation in 2023 and 2024 have only exacerbated this issue. More than half in the survey in 2017 indicated "salaries and other compensation from our church simply do not provide a strong enough financial base for our family."[22]

This financial pressure has a real impact on a marriage. It moves to a core issue of security. When a pastor's wife is living under the pressure of financial shortfall, she is living with a lack of security that will take its toll on relationships. Sometimes, it brings an anxiety that every member of the family feels.

Compensation is also a matter of respect. When a pastor is paid poorly, he and his wife can feel undervalued. In fact, the Bible uses the word *honor* to describe pastoral compensation in 1 Timothy 5:17. The word speaks to worth, to both remuneration and respect. A pastor and his wife can feel undervalued and disrespected when they are underpaid. This can have an impact on how they relate to the work.

One unseen way, pastor's wife, you can serve your husband is helping him to see the importance of communicating with the church family in regard to compensation. As a twenty-five-year-old pastor with a second baby on the way, my wife, Julie, and I found ourselves with no insurance. My wife got on the phone with what is today known as GuideStone, the entity I'm privileged to now lead, and gathered information about benefits and compensation planning.

I gathered up my courage and I went to talk to the leaders of the church I was pastoring, a church of fifty or sixty souls, a country church. I talked to them about our need, and we discussed the finances of the church. I asked them to cover both my health insurance and life insurance. They went and talked about it. The result? They covered my health insurance and life insurance and then put 10 percent of my salary into a retirement account. I can remember how good that felt. I felt valued as a pastor—as did Julie as a pastor's wife—and I realized my work meant something to them.

Not only do I remember how good it felt for the church to affirm me in that way, I also remember how nervous I was when I brought this to the church's attention. Financial matters are a challenge to address, there is no doubt about it.

But it's not just about your financial security. One day, if the Lord tarries, you and your husband will be called away to another place of vocational service or to vocational retirement. These difficult conversations aren't just a business discussion—they're a matter of discipleship, a matter that will hopefully pay dividends for your pastoral successors.

If you're a pastor's wife nudging your pastor-husband to become informed on these matters, we have a ton of free resources at GuideStone.org/pastor to help. Taking them prayerfully before key leaders is a way to serve unseen that will benefit him, you, your family, and future staff at the church as well.

Pastor's wife, you are a key part of your husband's ministry, whether God has called you to additional ministries beyond your family and the church or not. Serving unseen may not be glamorous, but whether your church family notices, whether your husband remembers to acknowledge it or not, you can be sure your Father in heaven sees it all and remembers.

And He will bless you for it.

Too many pastors' wives allow the burdens of their complex task to get the best of them. Over the years, she can feel unappreciated, empty, and jaded toward the very people her husband is called to shepherd. Psalm 134, the psalm for unseen saints, is good medicine for her soul. When her work is unappreciated, she embraces unseen service. When the demands of the role drain her, she replenishes her soul in private and public worship. When bitterness toward the people threatens to derail essential relationships, she sings Psalm 134 and commits to be a blessing to the community of faith in which she serves.

Chapter 6

The Good News for Unseen Servants

Call to Evening Worship

A song of ascents.

Now bless the LORD,
all you servants of the LORD
who stand in the LORD's house at night!
Lift up your hands in the holy place
and bless the LORD!

May the LORD,
Maker of heaven and earth,
bless you from Zion.
Psalm 134

David George was a powerful kingdom leader. Just after the Revolutionary War, he left Georgia with a few hundred people and sailed to Nova Scotia. He lived there for ten years under significant persecution while founding the first Baptist church of Shelbourne. He planted the church in the face of threats, arson fires, and other real danger. But he wasn't finished.

Pastor George migrated to West Africa in 1792. He became one of the founding fathers of Freetown, Sierra Leone. Of course, his passion for the gospel traveled to Africa with him. He planted the first Baptist church in West Africa. What an impact this man had for the gospel.

George was born in Essex County, Virginia, in the early 1740s. His parents were enslaved persons, John and Judith, who had been born in Africa. He experienced terrible cruelty as a child and adolescent. When he was around nineteen years of age, he escaped slavery. He ran away from Virginia and lived with the Natchez Native American tribe.

Eventually, David George came to live and work on the estate of George Galphin. The plantation was called Silver Bluff, and there was a preacher there named George Liele who introduced David George to Christ. We are blessed to have David George's testimony in his own words:

> (George Liele preached) Come unto me all ye that labor, are heavy laden, and I will give you rest. When it was ended I went to him and told him that I was weary and heavy laden and that the grace of God had given me rest.[23]

What a story!

Do you have a story like that? It is possible to work every day for a Christian ministry, yet never experience a life-changing encounter with Jesus Christ. **Your service does not save you.**

Do you have a good news story like David George? I was weary and burdened, but now God has given me rest. I was lost, but now I am found. I was doomed, but Jesus saved me. Every good news story has a beginning, a middle, and an end. Read Paul's beautiful summary of the good news of Jesus:

> For we too were once foolish, disobedient, deceived, enslaved by various passions and

> pleasures, living in malice and envy, hateful, detesting one another. But when the kindness of God our Savior and his love for mankind appeared, he saved us—not by works of righteousness that we had done, but according to his mercy—through the washing of regeneration and renewal by the Holy Spirit. He poured out his Spirit on us abundantly through Jesus Christ our Savior so that, having been justified by his grace, we may become heirs with the hope of eternal life. (Titus 3:3–7)

The beginning of our story is the same. We are bound by sin. The Bible describes the life of each one of us without Christ. We are foolish, disobedient, deceived, and enslaved. Wow! No wonder we are weary. Notice the progression of sin, or maybe the digression of sin: Sin always takes us farther and farther from all that is good—foolish, then disobedient, deceived, and enslaved. We do not meddle with sin; we are mastered by it.

Jesus told a story about a young man who was dominated by sin. This son was foolish, disobedient, deceived, and enslaved by his own passions and pleasures. He took all that his father so graciously gave to him and traveled far away only to waste it. Finally, he found himself desperately aware of his own brokenness. In the Bible, the parable says the prodigal son "came to his senses" (Luke 15:17 ESV). Literally, the language reads, "he came to himself."

We cannot come to Jesus until we come to ourselves. We need grace, sometimes tough grace, to see ourselves honestly, accurately. We all start in the same condition, the beginning of every person's story is the same: bound by sin, broken.

Sometimes church workers can live with a false sense of self. If we are not clear-eyed, we might make the mistake of assuming that working for a Christian ministry balances out any sin we might commit. We will never have a gospel story until we come to our senses and realize how bound by sin we are: "For all have sinned and fall short of the glory of God. . . . For the wages of sin is death" (Rom. 3:23; 6:23a).

Have you ever come to the end of yourself? Like David George, "I am weary, burdened, I need a Savior." This brings us to Act Two of the story.

Our beginning is bound by sin. The middle of our story can be summarized by one powerful word: *saved*. He saved us. I love the simplicity and clarity of this language. The Titus text printed earlier is one long, complex sentence, fifty-nine words in the original text. Much of this Bible text seems difficult to grasp, but one part stands out bright and clear: He saved us.

Notice the repetition of the thought. God is called God our Savior in verse 4. Jesus is called Savior in verse 6. The Lord does many good things for us when we come to Him by faith, but Paul puts the spotlight on one central reality. *He* saves us. It is His saving work, not ours.

The text makes it clear that the good news is *not* about what we do for God. This story is not about our character or conduct but about the saving work of God in Christ Jesus—His kindness, His love, His mercy, His grace.

Hudson Taylor was a great missionary. He and his family sacrificed much to advance the good news into the Inland of China. Soon after his first wife died, he wrote a letter to some of his children. His burden was that his children would have their own saving faith in Jesus. Just as it is not enough to work in a church or ministry, it is not enough to be a missionary kid. We each need our own story of faith in Jesus. Consider Hudson Taylor's appeal:

> I wish you, my precious children, knew what it was to give your hearts to Jesus to keep every day. I used to try to keep my own heart right, but it would be always going wrong; and so at last I had to give up trying myself and accept Jesus' offer to keep it for me. Don't you think that is the best way?[24]

Everyone is broken by sin, and everyone needs the saving power of Jesus.

Paul uses a beautiful word to describe God's saving work in Christ Jesus. The word speaks to a light shining in the darkness: *appeared*. "But when the kindness of God our Savior and his love for mankind appeared, he saved us" (Titus 3:4–5a). Bound by sin we sit captive in darkness until His light shines on us.

Why would the apostle Paul use the word *appeared* to describe God's saving work in our lives through Jesus Christ? Think. Paul is hinting at his own story. Paul shares his testimony three times in the book of Acts. He was foolish, disobedient, deceived, and enslaved by malice. He was hateful and hating others. In fact, he was on the road to Damascus to persecute the Christians there when Jesus intervened. A brilliant light from heaven suddenly flashed all around him and he fell to the ground, blind. Then he heard a voice.

It was the voice of Jesus, the risen Lord. That day, by grace, kindness, and love Jesus saved Saul of Tarsus. Paul's testimony was forever clear: "He saved me." He came as a light shining in the darkness of my sin. What a story!

Do you have a story like that? Can you say with confidence, "I was bound by sin, but Jesus saved me"? Wouldn't it fill you with forever regret if you spent years of your life, hour upon hour, working in a Christian ministry without ever experiencing the saving power of Jesus Christ? Let's press in a bit further to understand the ending of the gospel story.

What does it mean to be saved? After we see the light of Jesus, and stand in the light of His saving power, where do we stand? Our Titus text makes it clear. The vocabulary of the text is a bit technical, and the sentence structure is challenging, but the message is actually simple. When Jesus saves us, He makes us new, He makes us right, and He makes us forever His.

Paul describes this new life: through the washing of regeneration and renewal by the Holy Spirit. The Bible speaks of one event, one activity, one preposition governs this whole statement. When He saves us, the Holy Spirit washes us and makes us new. Regeneration and renewal are the gospel promise. This is a promise as old as Ezekiel.

> "I will also sprinkle clean water on you, and you will be clean. I will cleanse you from all your impurities and all your idols. I will give you a new heart and put a new spirit within you; I will remove your heart of stone and give you a heart of flesh. I will place my Spirit within you and cause you to follow my statutes and carefully observe my ordinances." (Ezek. 36:25–27)

John the Baptist echoed Ezekiel's promise when he identified Jesus as the Messiah: "I baptize you with water for repentance, but the one who is coming after me is more powerful than I. . . . He himself will baptize you with the Holy Spirit and fire" (Matt. 3:11). Now, Paul uses baptismal language to describe this same promise of life change (Titus 3:5). When

Jesus saves us, He makes us new, a new creation; old things are passed away! We are so broken and bound by sin that we do not need a new set of rules; we cannot follow the rules. We do not need a new schedule; we cannot keep a schedule. We need a new heart. Has Jesus made you new?

When Jesus saves us and makes us right, we are justified by His grace. Here Paul uses legal language (v. 7). We were wrong, guilty, condemned. We were not right with God, but in Christ Jesus, we have been made right.

This is that concept that Hudson Taylor was using in his letter. We cannot make ourselves right; we cannot keep ourselves right. But Jesus justifies us by His grace.

Justification meets our primary spiritual need. We stand guilty, under God's righteous judgment. The guilt is a burden because we know that we are not right with God. We have no peace. The gospel offers us freedom from that guilt through the work of Jesus on the cross. He paid our sin debt; He took on the condemnation that we deserve.

Notice the settled reality described by the verb tense, "having been justified by his grace" (v. 7). As followers of Jesus, we do not just hope to be right with God one day, maybe. We have been justified. Oh, the joy that comes from knowing, from saying with confidence, "I have been justified by His grace."

We have a twofold problem as the result of our sin, according to theologian Millard Erickson: our nature is corrupt, and our moral character is polluted.[25] Thus, we need Jesus to make us new. Yet, the other aspect of our sin nature remains. We are guilty.

We are liable to be punished for our willful transgressions. It is this problem of our guilt that justification addresses. "Justification is God's action pronouncing sinners righteous in his sight."[26] How can a sinner like me be accepted by a holy God? The answer is justification. Jesus paid the penalty for our sins on the cross to set us right with God. "Therefore, having been justified by faith, we have peace with God through our Lord Jesus Christ" (Rom. 5:1 NASB). "He made Him who knew no sin to be sin on our behalf, so that we might become the righteousness of God in Him" (2 Cor. 5:21 NASB). When Jesus saves us, He makes us new (regeneration), and He makes us right (justification).

When Jesus saves us, He makes us His. We are His heirs. "So that, having been justified by his grace, we may become heirs with the hope of eternal life" (Titus 3:7). Anytime the

Bible speaks of our hope of eternal life, we tend to think about our future in heaven. However, Paul makes more than a promise of heaven someday in the future. He is making a present promise. We are His heirs.

Unseen servants are heirs, just like their pastors and the church members they serve! Heirs are sons and daughters. This is the language of adoption. When God saves us in Christ Jesus, He adopts us as His children. In our sins, we are alienated and alone, separated from God. In Christ Jesus, we belong to His family. We are His—forever. The New Testament abounds with the language of adoption:

> But to all who did receive him, he gave them the right to be children of God, to those who believe in his name. (John 1:12)

> For all those led by God's Spirit are God's sons. For you did not receive a spirit of slavery to fall back into fear. Instead, you received the Spirit of adoption, by whom we cry out, "*Abba*, Father!" The Spirit himself testifies together with our spirit that we are God's children. (Rom. 8:14–16)

> To redeem those under the law, so that we might receive adoption as sons. And because you are sons, God sent the Spirit of his Son into our hearts, crying, "*Abba*, Father!" So, you are no longer a slave but a son, and if a son, then God has made you an heir. (Gal. 4:5–7)

Notice that to be an heir is to have been adopted. An unseen servant isn't just a worker but an adopted member of God's family.

The Westminster Confession of Faith has a wonderful description of adoption:

> All those that are justified, God vouchsafeth, in and for His only Son Jesus Christ, to make partakers of the grace of adoption: by which they are taken into the number, and enjoy the liberties and privileges of the children of God; have His name put upon them; receive the Spirit of adoption; have access to the throne of grace with boldness; are enabled to cry, Abba, Father; are pitied, protected,

> provided for, and chastened by Him as by a father; yet never cast off, but sealed to the day of redemption, and inherit the promises, as heirs of everlasting salvation.

Hallelujah!

J. I. Packer calls adoption the "highest privilege that the gospel offers."[27] He suggests justification is conceived in terms of law, viewing God as judge, while adoption is conceived in terms of love, viewing God as father. To be an heir is to be included forever as family.

> See what great love the Father has given us
> that we should be called God's children—
> and we are! (1 John 3:1a)

When Jesus saves us, when He shines like a light in our darkness, He brings blessings that seem too good to be true. He meets the deep longing of our hearts. Jesus makes us new through His Holy Spirit power of renewal and regeneration. He makes us right, justified by His grace through His finished work of the cross. He makes us forever His, adopted into His family as sons and daughters. Wow! This is good news.

Let me tell you my story. I was foolish, disobedient, deceived, enslaved by sin, but Jesus saved me. He made me new; He made me right; He made me His.

This was also Paul's story, and the story of David George. It is the gospel story. Is it your story? How tragic it would be to spend your life working for a church or Christian ministry without a personal relationship with Jesus Christ. Everyone needs a story of their personal encounter with Christ.

You could come to yourself right now, and come to Jesus as Savior. Express your heart to the Lord like this:

Oh Lord Jesus, I see now that I am a sinner, broken and bound. I cannot do enough or know enough or work enough to make myself right. Forgive me of my sin. I believe, Jesus, that You died on the cross for my sins, and that You rose again to reign as the Lord of all. Jesus, I ask You to save me. Please, Lord, make me new, make me right, make me Yours. Amen.

Not far north and a little west of the Dallas metropolitan area is a little village called Tioga, Texas. If you passed through on the highway, you would miss an old church with a historical marker:

> The Lone Star Primitive Baptist Church was organized in 1893. Present church built, 1948. T. N. Cutler, first pastor. Sam Rayburn, Speaker, U. S. House of Representatives was baptized here 1956, by H. G. Ball, Elder. Ball conducted Rayburn's funeral in Bonham, 1961. Four presidents attended.

Sam Rayburn was a United States Congressman from Texas from 1913 to 1961. He was the Speaker of the House for seventeen of those years. He was one of the most powerful political forces of his day. Sam Rayburn died in office at age seventy-nine in 1961. About five years before his death, on September 24, 1956, Jesus saved Sam Rayburn.

The elder of the church, a grocer named Henry Greer Ball, asked at the end of the worship service if anyone would like to accept Jesus Christ as Savior. Up stepped seventy-four-year-old Sam Rayburn, Speaker of the House. This was such a big deal that the local newspaper reported the story.

"Then, wearing socks, trousers, and a white shirt, the Speaker of the House was completely immersed for a moment in a portable baptistry before he emerged, dripping wet, to hear himself baptized in the name of the Father, the Son, and the Holy Ghost."[28] The congregation of about forty people broke into song"

> How sweet the name of Jesus sounds in a believer's
> ear!
> It soothes his sorrows, heals his wounds, and
> drives away his fear.[29]

Sam Rayburn had a story too. It is the story of a powerful politician who was so humbled by his own sin, his own need for a Savior, that he stripped down to his shirt sleeves and stocking feet and crawled into a portable tank in front of that small group of common folk. His actions proclaimed his story.

I am foolish, disobedient, deceived, enslaved by sin, but Jesus has saved me. He made me new; He made me right; He made me His.

Paul, the Hebrew of Hebrews who meticulously kept the finest letter of the law; David George, a runaway slave in the backwoods of Georgia; the missionary kids of Hudson Taylor;

and the Speaker of the House, Sam Rayburn—they all have the same story.

What's your story?

Pride is deadly. Pride can plague religious workers. Unseen servants who work hard for a church or ministry, are especially susceptible to their vision being clouded and not seeing themselves clearly. Maybe such a servant imagines that her job justifies her before God. Bible truth and Christian talk abound, leading the unseen servant to assume he is spiritually okay. *Watch out!* Everyone has the same story: broken sinners in need of a faithful Savior who alone can make them new.

Jesus told a parable that every ministry worker needs to keep front of mind. Allow me to paraphrase.

Two men went up to the church to pray, one worked for the church and the other worked in a local business. The man who worked at the church stood tall and prayed out loud, "Lord, I am just as good as the people who come in and out of this building every week. I don't waste my work in the world, but I work hard for the church. I help these old people, I clean up the messes the children make, I am never around bad language and dishonest deals. I willingly make less money than others because I am working in this church. Compared to most people, I am not too bad."

Meanwhile, the other man, the one who came to church on his lunch break from business, bowed down low between the pews. With hands tight-fisted against his chest, he whispered, "Oh Father, have mercy on me, a broken sinner. Save me, through the finished work of Jesus on the cross. I need You to make me new, make me right, please, make me forever Yours!"

This broken-down sinner has a gospel story.

Remember early in our study we discovered that Psalm 134 calls on each one of us to bless God in worship and to seek God's blessing on our lives. So blessing flows from man to God, and blessing flows from God to man:

> Now bless the Lord,
> all you servants of the Lord
> who stand in the Lord's house at night!
> Lift up your hands in the holy place
> and bless the Lord!
>
> May the Lord,
> Maker of heaven and earth,
> bless you from Zion.

Surely, there is a difference between what I do when I bless the Lord in worship and what He does when He blesses me by His grace.

The scholar Derek Kidner gave us insight: "The exchange is quite unequal: to bless God is to acknowledge gratefully what He is; but to bless man, God must make of him what he is not, and give him what he has not."[30]

The good news of Jesus Christ is that "unequal exchange." All I can do for God is to honestly acknowledge Him for who He is. He is kind, He is Savior who shed His blood on the cross for our sins. He is full of love; He is merciful and full of grace (to use the vocabulary of Titus 3).

What does He do to bless me? My Savior gives me what I could never earn and does for me what I could never do for myself. He saves me.

This is the good news for everyone, including unseen servants.

Afterword

At first blush, it might seem odd to have the president of one of the nation's largest church benefits boards write *this* book. After all, we seem to be focused on church leaders who stand on the platform and proclaim the mysteries of the Lord's kingdom from His book or lead in some other public face of ministry.

When I came to GuideStone, I assembled a team of our leaders, from among both our staff and our trustees, to reframe our mission and vision for this next era of GuideStone's service. The vision we adopted is simple: Every servant of Christ finishes well. A vision statement should be aspirational, simple, and one we'll have to work diligently toward if we're ever to achieve it.

We chose the wording very specifically. We want *every servant* of Christ to finish well. Every servant: pastors, ministers, missionaries, musicians, media team members, communications professionals, janitors, custodians, chefs, cooks, security personnel—if you serve in a local church, you are a servant of Christ. And we want you to finish well.

Our mission is to enhance financial security and resilience for those who serve Christ—for seen servants and for the unseen as well! Resilience is the capacity to bounce back. Resilience is connected to the biblical call to persevere. The advance of the gospel message depends on the resilience of those serving in gospel ministries. At the heart of the mission is a conviction that financial security is a key factor in resilience. Those who want to stay in the work over the long haul must pay attention to their financial wellness.

It's important to note: You can't finish well unless you first start well. And then you must stay well over the course of your ministry—and yes, even if your job is operational, even if you never stepped foot on a seminary campus, your job is a ministry.

Start Well

In a perfect world, you start preparing for vocational retirement on day one of your career. For many of us, that doesn't happen for one reason or another. It's been said the best time to plant a tree was thirty years ago; the second-best time to plant is today. So, whether we caught you early in your career or not, start now. Get on a budget, start saving for rainy days, and invest toward retirement. If you serve in a Southern Baptist church and receive W-2 reportable income, you can participate in our 403(b)(9) Retirement Plan for Southern Baptist Churches—the Church Retirement Plan. If you're in a church or ministry eligible to participate with GuideStone, we can serve you in a plan designed for your ministry. Most of the five hundred people who serve at GuideStone do so in an unseen manner, so we uniquely understand your point of view and your needs!

Stay Well

We want you to stay well—relationally, professionally, and financially. Relationally, you need to stay plugged into the Lord and His work in your life. As we discussed previously, it's all too easy to put our focus on the task at hand and lose sight of the One for whom we ultimately work. Don't lose sight of that. Don't lose sight of the relationships with your family. Too many ministers, too many workers, get to the end of their career, having achieved their goals, only to find their families—spouses, kids, grandchildren, and extended family members—are virtual strangers. We want you to have good health and good relationships.

And we want you to stay well on your health journey—taking time for proper rest, nutrition, and regular exercise will protect your physical, emotional, and mental health. Your spiritual health should be a focus, as well, of course. Block off time for worship, Bible study, and prayer.

Staying well on your financial journey means growing your savings, making sure you have the proper estate plan in place. Did you get a late start on retirement planning? There are tools available to you such as "age 50 catchup contributions," which can help mitigate the effects of that late start.

Finish Well

To finish well is about freedom. Those who finish well make it to retirement years with freedom from the anxiety of financial pressure. We may not be wealthy, but we are not burdened with worries about money. As one pastor recently reported: "I am doing just fine." To finish well is to live in your later years free from anxiety and free for service.

Imagine being financially free to serve Christ in new ways. While serving Christ, you are gaining some skill and expertise. You will always want to use that expertise to help the people of God. Imagine having the financial freedom to serve a smaller church as a volunteer or to mentor those who come along behind you. Maybe you can help a church plant or serve in short-term mission assignments. Financial security gives you the freedom to serve.

I have a picture in my mind's eye of the quintessential unseen servant: He or she served faithfully and saved sacrificially. The unseen servant contributed to the kingdom in ways that no one, not even he or she, recognizes. God alone knows the impact of service. That servant has reached that place of vocational retirement. He isn't bitter or greedy. In fact, he is loved by colleagues and the few members who truly know his work. Maybe the church brings him and his family onto the platform to receive recognition. And he enters retirement, healthy, with a family that is glad to have him around and in a financial situation where he can enjoy the fruits of his labor.

That's not the stuff of made-for-TV movies or lottery winners alone. It can be your future if you start well.

GuideStone Is Here for Unseen Servants

You may have heard we're here for pastors and ministers. That is certainly true! We're here for you as well! In fact, 23,000 members we serve are office personnel in a church; more than 5,000 are in a custodial position, and another 6,400 people work as church school or day school workers. We care about all of God's servants and want to see you start well, stay well, and ultimately, to finish well for God's glory and your good. Visit our website, GuideStone.org, to learn how to get started. Your future self will thank you for making time today.

Epilogue

Mission:Dignity

Most people we serve through Mission:Dignity served unseen. Many of them served as pastors or pastors' wives away from the spotlight, unseen to a watching world.

Except to God. To Him and His people, their service mattered.

Mission:Dignity helps more than 2,800 individuals every year with extra money needed for housing, food, and vital medications. It also ensures a well-deserved dignity, independence, and, often, the ability to continue serving the Lord.

Let me share three of the thousands of stories we hear from those we serve.

Mike and Sandra Dowling worked for the Social Security Administration (SSA) in Birmingham, Alabama, for many years. "She made more money than I did," recalls Mike in a jovial tone, "I remember this to keep myself humble."

Ever-present in church life beyond the daily grind, Mike was licensed and ordained, serving as a deacon in a local church before he felt the call to preach.

Mike attended school at night, receiving his bachelor's and seminary degrees before shepherding his first church. The Dowlings soon quit their jobs at the SSA, sold their house, and moved into the parsonage of Brighton Baptist Church. "I don't believe it's an accident where God leads me in the Scriptures," said Mike, "and Almighty God turned me to Mark 10:27–30 (CSB) at this crucial time in our lives":

> Looking at them, Jesus said, "With man it is impossible, but not with God, because all things are possible with God."
>
> Peter began to tell him, "Look, we have left everything and followed you."
>
> "Truly I tell you," Jesus said, "there is no one who has left house or brothers or sisters or mother or father or children or fields for my sake and for the sake of the gospel, who will not receive a hundred times more, now at this time—houses, brothers and sisters,

> mothers and children, and fields, with persecutions—and eternal life in the age to come."

Even though they left all they'd known behind, the Dowlings chose to follow the Lord's leading.

Several years later, they were called to another church and another parsonage, but while serving there, their home was deliberately burned down to the ground. The local authorities declared it arson. The Dowlings soldiered on and served regardless, holding fast to the promises in Mark 10. As their time of ministry at that church came to a close and retirement loomed, they were at a loss as to where to go.

"Leeds Housing Authority came to my attention—a housing project located just outside Birmingham," remembers Mike. "We moved there not really knowing exactly what we were going to do. I was preaching at churches here and there, but all of a sudden, I began to look around me and see needs. There are 158 apartments in the project. People were hungry, they had needs, and they needed prayer."

The Dowlings began to serve the community in any way they could: through food, spiritual counseling, handouts—whatever it took. Sponsored by local churches and Baptist associations, the Dowlings began to plant a church in the projects. "This is a seven-day-a-week, twenty-four-seven job," says Mike. "I have a pulpit on my front porch because people walk by and they say, 'Pray for us.' And I have the food there to give them," says Mike. "We take people to the hospital. We take people to the store. We take people to the bus stop. These people work. Sometimes, I have to give out the food at night because they're not there during the day. And we've served homeless people. We're right across from the strip and we're friends."

In 2018, Mission:Dignity stepped in to ensure that the Dowlings themselves are taken care of and free to serve the community without worrying about their finances.

"When we received news from Mission:Dignity that we were accepted and what we would receive monthly, it immediately freed me up to better serve this community. It would be very difficult, probably impossible, to do this ministry if Mission:Dignity was not there to help us," says Mike.

With the funds provided, the Dowlings have been able to buy needed kitchen appliances to help them serve food to the community, repair the cars they use to transport others, and even help pay for a life insurance policy to give them greater peace of mind as they age. "There are no words to describe what a difference Mission:Dignity has made in our lives," says Sandra.

Remembering the promises in Mark 10, Sandra says, "We left a house when we started and had another house burn down. All that prepared us for this ministry. We didn't realize that we wouldn't be going back. Those experiences put us where God wanted us—and we've never been happier."

The Dowlings know that their service may be unseen to the world, but it mattered to the Lord and was seen by Him whom they so faithfully served.

Ann Perry didn't expect to go into ministry halfway through her life. At forty, she lost her dear husband in a tragic accident, and after a time of great sorrow and mourning, she submitted her life to ministry. The Lord soon led her to volunteer with the Mount Zion Baptist Association of North Carolina (MZBA). Shortly after starting to volunteer, the association knew they had a gem of a worker, and they hired her full-time! Working for the MZBA for twenty-five years, Ms. Perry spent much of her time working with local food banks, truck stops, and prisons and witnessed the Lord move in many ways.

Ms. Perry always found new, innovative ways to minister to others and support the ministries in her charge. She started a thrift store that directly funded her association's food bank. As a result, they no longer had to rely on the state convention to purchase food. The Lord also used Ann to create a local truck-stop ministry. She and her teams saw passing truckers as an unreached demographic, so they started the "Right Turn Trucker's Chapel" at one of the local truck stops. Through this ministry, they were able to reach countless truck drivers with the gospel.

Outside of her association, Ann became very involved in prison ministry. She assisted her local prison chaplain in starting a toy store for children of inmates. In this way, Ms. Perry gave incarcerated fathers a chance to be dads to their kids during Christmastime. And right up until COVID-19, she hosted monthly birthday parties for the inmates. The gospel was preached and received many times at these events.

Now retired from the MZBA, Ann is still active in many of these ministries today because of the support she receives from Mission:Dignity. Without Mission:Dignity, she would not be able to support herself financially or continue to serve in this capacity. Ann wants all Mission:Dignity donors to know, "I have searched my vocabulary and cannot find words that adequately express how much I appreciate your generous gifts." Mission:Dignity has assisted Ms. Perry with new hearing aids, paid for dental work, and sends monthly grants that keep her living on mission for the sake of the kingdom.

Some of you may serve through ministries or associations of churches. That work can go very unnoticed by the world. But it is never forgotten by the Lord.

Elvis Durrill retired from the pastorate after thirty-six years to care for his wife the last six years of her life. Heart problems, then an episode of cancer, meant around-the-clock care, and Elvis soon found his savings depleted.

That's when he decided to apply for assistance himself. Approved in short order, Elvis is grateful for God's timing in helping him see the need to reach out to others about his situation.

"It's hard to ask for help," he confesses, "but God always takes care of me."

With his financial burdens being relieved through a Mission:Dignity grant, Elvis is able to focus on his new ministry—right over his back fence. "Every year I plant a vegetable garden in my backyard. I use my crop as a tool to witness to my neighbor."

It all started one summer as he was working in his garden. He noticed his next-door neighbor was struggling with starting his lawn mower.

"I picked a basket of red-ripe tomatoes and went to the fence to share. God used the garden and me to plant some spiritual seeds," he recalls.

Elvis saw his other next-door neighbor walk a similar path to his own—caring for a wife struggling with cancer. His service as a hospice chaplain and his own journey gave him the experience to walk alongside the neighbors, praying with and encouraging them. Once again, the garden opened the door.

"Every morning, I pray, 'Lord, help me today to be all that You want me to be,'" Elvis says. "The greatest blessing comes from knowing He is not through with me here on earth. There is no end to the opportunities to serve."

Grateful to the Mission:Dignity ministry for what it has enabled him to do, Elvis recently told us, "I cannot put into words what is in my heart. You have helped me through a very difficult time. God bless you!"

"If I had one request of the Lord, I would pray if it was His will that I meet, rejoice with, and shake the hands of the people God is using in this ministry," Elvis wrote.

Elvis understands the ministry of presence in his neighborhood. Once again, this is an example of someone who serves well, even without the recognition of others. But his service does not go unnoticed by the Lord.

All author royalties and proceeds from the sale of this book go to the benefit of Mission:Dignity, where 100 percent of the gifts go to help a retired Southern Baptist servant in need. An endowment covers all of the administrative expenses of the ministry. If you are a retired Southern Baptist pastor, minister, worker, or a widow of one, and you find it difficult to meet your monthly needs, please reach out. Or, if you know someone in need, you can refer someone, and we'll reach out to them. Simply visit MissionDignity.org to learn more. If God places it on your heart, you can also give through Mission:Dignity at the same website.

About the Author

Hance Dilbeck is president and chief executive officer of GuideStone. He joined GuideStone in July 2021 as president-elect and became president on March 1, 2022.

Dr. Dilbeck came to GuideStone from the position of executive director-treasurer of Oklahoma Baptists, where he served since 2018. Prior to that, he was a pastor in Oklahoma churches for thirty years. He and his wife, Julie, have three married sons and ten grandchildren.

Notes

1. "More Than 100,000 Fishing-Related Deaths Occur Each Year, Study Finds," Pew, December 14, 2022, https://www.pewtrusts.org/en/research-and-analysis/issue-briefs/2022/11/more-than-100000-fishing-related-deaths-occur-each-year-study-finds.

2. Christy Bieber, "10 Most Dangerous Jobs in America for 2024," Forbes, July 12, 2023, https://www.forbes.com/advisor/legal/workers-comp/most-dangerous-jobs-america/.

3. "Civilian occupations with high fatal work injury rates," U.S. Bureau of Labor Statistics, 2022, https://www.bls.gov/charts/census-of-fatal-occupational-injuries/civilian-occupations-with-high-fatal-work-injury-rates.htm.

4. Sara Weissman, "Northern Seminary President Resigns Amid Bullying Allegations," Inside Higher Ed, March 16, 2023, https://www.insidehighered.com/quicktakes/2023/03/17/northern-seminary-president-resigns-amid-bullying-allegations.

5. Daniel Payne, "Florida Church Employee Pleads Guilty to Defrauding Parish of $775,000," *Catholic News Agency*, May 30, 2024, https://www.catholicnewsagency.com/news/257844/florida-church-employee-pleads-guilty-to-defrauding-parish-of-775-dollars-000-cents.

6. "Vault: New Yorkers make a stink about 1981 garbage strike," ABC7NY, December 17, 2021, https://abc7ny.com/garbage-strike-1981-eyewitness-news-vault-archive/11349236/.

7. James D. G. Dunn, *Word Biblical Commentary: Romans 9–16* (Dallas: Word, 1988), 894.

8. Dunn, *Word Biblical Commentary, Romans 9–16*, 888.

9. *Merriam-Webster Dictionary*, s.v. "acknowledge, v.," accessed August 27, 2024, https://www.merriam-webster.com/dictionary/acknowledge.

10. Mission:Dignity, a ministry within GuideStone, provides financial assistance to retired Southern Baptist ministers, workers, and widows struggling to meet basic needs. Learn more at MissionDignity.org.

11. Thomas D. Lea, *God's Transforming Word: The Holy Bible: How to Study Your Bible* (Nashville: LifeWay Christian Resources, 2000).

12. https://www.studylight.org/commentaries/eng/mac/psalms-134.html

13. Derek Kidner, *Psalms 73–150* (Downers Grove, IL: InterVarsity, 2008), 490.

14. Kidner, *Psalms 73–150,* 490.

15. Barbara Haas et al., "Close to home: An analysis of the relationship between location of residence and location of injury," National Library of Medicine, April 2018, https://ncbi.nlm.nih.gov/pmc/articles/PMC4375775/.

16. Elena A. Nikitina, "Is Selfie Behavior Related to Psychological Well-Being?" September 15, 2021, https://www.ncbi.nlm.nih.gov/pmc/articles/PMC9887880/#:~:text=Research%20has%20confirmed%20that%20the,seeking%20self%2Dapproval%2C%20maintaining%20a.

17. Marva J. Dawn, *How Shall We Worship? Biblical Guidelines for the Worship Wars* (Eugene, OR: Wipf and Stock, 2015), xi.

18. Thomas Watson, *The Godly Man's Picture: Drawn with a Scripture Pencil* (1666; repr. ed., Zeeland, MI: Reformed Church Publications, 2009), 125.

19. "Survey of American Pastors' Spouses," Lifeway Research, September 12, 2017, https://research.lifeway.com/wp-content/uploads/2017/09/Pastor-Spouse-Quantitative-Report-Sept-2017.pdf.

20. "Marcos Urbina's Story: A Reluctant Call; a Resolute Response," GuideStone, https://www.guidestone.org/Resources/Education/Articles/Mission-Dignity/A-Reluctant-Call-A-Resounding-Response-Marcos-Urbina.

21. "Pastor Spouse Research Study," Lifeway Research, https://research.lifeway.com/wp-23. content/uploads/2017/09/Pastor-Spouse-Research-Report-Sept-2017.pdf, accessed August 27, 2024.

22. "Pastor Spouse Research Study," Lifeway Research, https://research.lifeway.com/wp-23. content/uploads/2017/09/Pastor-Spouse-Research-Report-Sept-2017.pdf, accessed August 27, 2024.

23. David T. Shannon, ed., *George Liele's Life and Legacy: An Unsung Hero* (Macon, GA: Mercer University Press, 2012), 142.

24. Dr. and Mrs. Howard Taylor, *The Growth of a Work of God: Hudson Taylor and the China Inland Mission*, vol. 2 (OMF International, 1919), 204.

25. Millard J. Erickson, *Christian Theology* (Grand Rapids: Baker Academic, 2013), 883.

26. Erickson, *Christian Theology,* 883.

27. J. I Packer, *Knowing God* (Downers Grove: InterVarsity Press, 2023).

28. https://theparisnews.com/news/bonham-s-sam-rayburn-baptized-at-age-74-found-himself-immersed-in-national-controversy/article_23f0aff0-cccc-11e7-b6f5-ab66adfd0d40.html

29. John Newton, "How Sweet the Name of Jesus Sounds" (1779), public domain.

30. Derek Kidner, *Psalms 73–150* (Downers Grove, IL: InterVarsity, 2008), 490.